QUICK & EASY
MICROWAVING™
CHICKEN

Developed By The Kitchens Of The MICROWAVE COOKING INSTITUTE ™

Copyright © 1986 by Cy DeCosse Incorporated
5900 Green Oak Drive
Minnetonka, Minnesota 55343
All rights reserved.
Library of Congress Catalog Card No. 86-16611

Library of Congress Cataloging-in-Publication Data

Quick & Easy Microwaving Chicken.

Includes index. 1. Cookery (Chicken) 2. Microwave Cookery.
I. Title: Quick & Easy Microwaving Chicken.
TX750.Q53   1986   641.6'65   86-16611
ISBN 0-86573-526-3
ISBN 0-86573-528-1 (pbk.)

Published by Prentice Hall Press
A Division of Simon & Schuster, Inc., New York
ISBN 0-13-749391-6

Contents

Simple Saucy Chicken 14

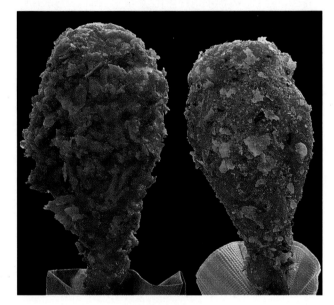

Poultry 4

Super Convenience 6

Chicken Basics 8

Quick Coatings for
Chicken Pieces 18

Chicken Pieces 10

Chicken Breasts 26

Whole Chickens 42

Creative Leftovers 70

Soups & Stews 52

Make Ahead Meals 78

Salads 62

No Time to Cook? 90

Poultry

The microwave is revolutionizing the way America cooks and eats poultry. The delicious, complete chicken main dishes that were once reserved for Sundays and holidays can now be prepared with fast-food ease anytime you want. Cooking times are cut by up to 50%, and the lean, low-fat meat stays moist and tender without tedious basting. As a bonus, you'll find that leftovers reheated in your microwave oven are as juicy and flavorful as the original meal.

From Sweet-and-Sour Chicken in about 15 minutes, to a classic Herb-roasted Chicken in just 25 minutes, welcome to *Quick & Easy Microwaving Chicken*, a collection of more than 70 easy recipes and more than 100 clear color photos designed to make *your* microwave oven perform the way you want it to perform. At last.

How to Select Chicken

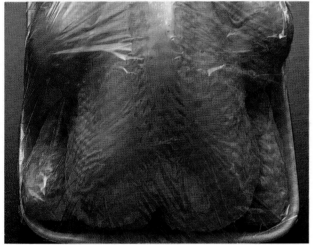

1 Choose plump broiler-fryers weighing about 2½ lbs. Look for smooth skin and a minimum of moisture in the package.

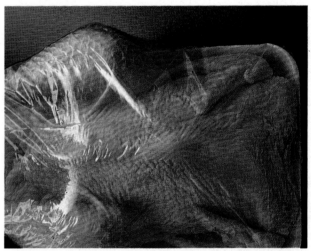

2 Avoid stewing hens and fryers with thick skin, large pores, or excess fat under the skin.

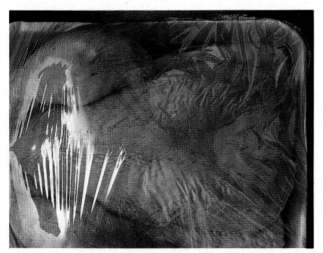

3 Check for large amounts of pink liquid in bag. This may indicate that fresh chicken has been frozen and thawed.

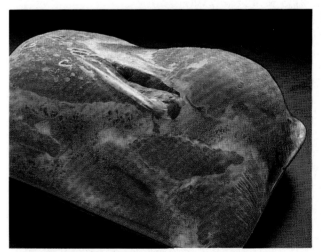

4 Inspect frozen chicken for freezer burn. Avoid packages containing pink ice; this indicates that poultry has been thawed and refrozen.

Super Convenience

Four options for maximum timesavings

Even when you have no time to cook or shop, you and your family still have to eat. Now you can extend the microwave advantage by choosing from a wide range of convenient, pre-cooked chicken products, available in canned, frozen or delicatessen form. Your microwave recipes will deliver complete, delicious, nutritious meals to the table in less time than it takes to run out for fast-food.

Canned chicken products offer relatively inexpensive long-term convenience. Available in a wide variety of forms — flaked, chunked, even whole birds — canned chicken is ideal for salads, soups, sandwiches and casseroles.

Deli chicken, available freshly cooked at most supermarkets, allows for creative cooking at a moment's notice. Broiled whole chickens or roasted pieces can be adapted for delicious glazed or barbecued recipes in just seconds.

Fresh turkey can be substituted in most recipes which use raw chicken, and some pre-cooked convenience turkey products are also available. Leftover roast turkey meat can be used whenever a recipe calls for chicken cubes or strips.

CONVENIENT SUBSTITUTES FOR COOKED CHICKEN

When Recipe Calls For:	Substitute:
1 cup cubed cooked chicken	1 can (5 oz.) chunk chicken
2 cups cubed cooked chicken	1 can (3 lb. 2 oz.) whole chicken deboned and cut up
2 to 2½ cups cubed cooked chicken	1 deli roast chicken (2½ to 3-lb.) deboned and cut up
3 cups cubed cooked chicken	1 pkg. (12 oz.) frozen diced chicken meat
4 cups cubed cooked chicken	1 lb. boneless deli chicken or turkey, or 1 pkg. (16 oz.) frozen diced turkey meat

Frozen poultry products include pre-cooked crispy-coated and uncoated pieces which are perfect for stews, hot dishes and barbecue recipes. Frozen chicken retains its fresh poultry taste for months, and defrosts in your microwave in just minutes.

Chicken Basics

How to Freeze Poultry

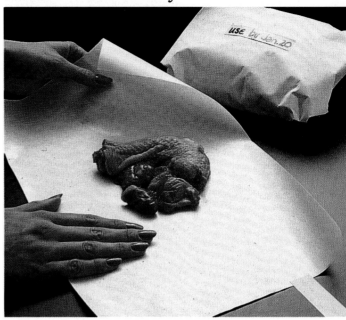

If properly stored, poultry will remain fresh up to 2 days in the refrigerator or 6 months in the freezer. To keep poultry fresh in the refrigerator, rinse with cold water, pat dry and wrap with plastic wrap. To freeze, wrap with an additional layer of freezer paper.

To defrost frozen chicken, microwave at 30% (Medium Low) for whole chickens, or at 50% (Medium) for chicken pieces. Rearrange chicken once during the defrosting time; chicken is defrosted as soon as the meat is cold but no longer icy.

1 Remove giblets and freeze separately if you plan to keep poultry longer than 3 months. Giblets will not keep as long as rest of bird.

How to Prepare Chicken for Microwaving

1 Wash chicken in cold water and remove the excess fat. Pat chicken dry.

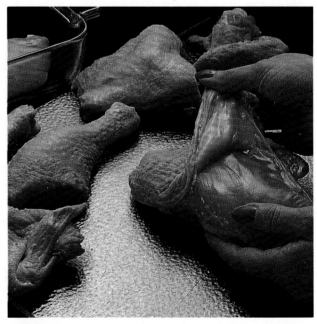

2 Remove chicken skin for low-fat preparation; microwaved chicken will stay moist, even without the skin.

2 Freeze poultry parts in the original package if you plan on using it within two weeks.

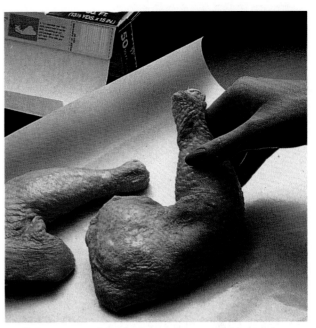

3 Remove poultry from package and wrap in coated freezer paper, or overwrap package with foil for longer storage.

How to Test Microwave Chicken for Doneness

1 Whole birds are done when legs move freely at joints, meat near the bone is no longer pink and the juices run clear. Internal temperature of meaty portion of thigh should be 185°F.

2 Poultry parts are done when meat near the bone is no longer pink. With boneless cuts, juices should run clear.

Chicken Pieces

These versatile & economical poultry cuts can be used in dozens of recipes

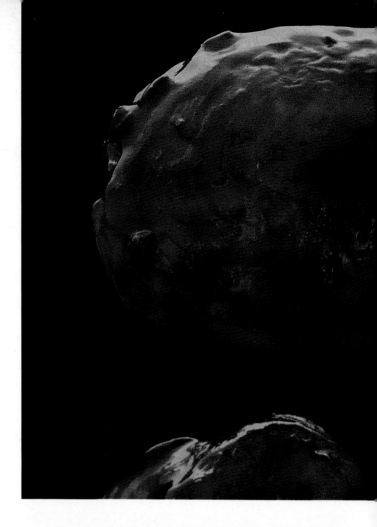

One of the best bargains in microwaving is a meal featuring fresh chicken pieces. Buy a whole broiler-fryer and divide it yourself for greatest economy, or choose packages of pre-cut thighs, drumsticks or breasts. Extra portions or leftovers can be used in soups, stews, salads, oriental dishes and casseroles.

Microwave at High:	Time:
¼ chicken (2 pieces)	6-9 minutes
½ chicken (4 pieces)	9-12 minutes

How to Microwave Chicken Pieces

1 Arrange chicken with meatiest portions toward outside edges of dish. If desired, season with pinch of dried parsley flakes or tarragon leaves.

2 Cover dish with plastic wrap vented at one edge of dish. Microwave for ½ of cooking time as directed in chart (above).

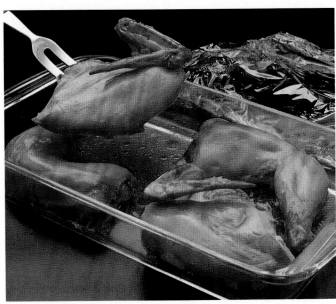

3 Rearrange chicken so less-cooked areas are toward outside edges. Re-cover and microwave for remaining time, or until meat near bone is no longer pink and juices run clear.

Brush chicken pieces with barbecue sauce, soy sauce or teriyaki sauce before microwaving and when rearranging pieces, if desired.

Simple Saucy Chicken

*Simple recipes to add zest
to traditional chicken dishes*

◄ Barbecued Chicken Drumsticks

¾ cup catsup
¼ cup chopped onion
2 tablespoons water
2 tablespoons chopped celery
1 tablespoon vinegar
1 teaspoon Worcestershire sauce
1 teaspoon sugar
½ teaspoon dry mustard
¼ teaspoon liquid smoke flavoring
⅛ teaspoon pepper
8 chicken drumsticks (2 lbs.), skin removed

4 servings

1 Combine all ingredients, except drumsticks, in a 4-cup measure. Cover with wax paper. Microwave at High for 3 minutes, or until hot, stirring once during cooking time.

2 Microwave at 50% (Medium) for 13 to 19 minutes longer, or until the vegetables are tender and the flavors are blended, stirring 2 or 3 times during cooking.

3 Arrange the drumsticks in a 9-inch square baking dish with meaty ends toward outside edges. Brush with ⅓ of the sauce. Cover with wax paper. Microwave at High for 7 minutes.

4 Turn over and rearrange drumsticks; brush with the remaining sauce. Re-cover. Microwave at High for 6 to 9 minutes, or until meat near the bone is no longer pink and the juices run clear.

Total Cooking Time: 29 to 38 minutes

Outdoor Barbecued Chicken Pieces

2½ to 3-lb. whole broiler-fryer chicken, cut into 8 pieces
Prepared barbecue sauce

4 servings

1 Arrange chicken pieces in a 10-inch square baking dish, with bony-sides down and thick portions toward outside of the dish. Cover with wax paper.

2 Microwave at High for 10 minutes, turning and rearranging pieces once during cooking time.

3 Place chicken on charcoal grill over hot coals. Baste chicken with your favorite barbecue sauce. Grill for 15 to 20 minutes, or until meat near the bone is no longer pink, and the juices run clear.

Total Cooking Time: 25 to 30 minutes

Quick & Easy Sauce Ideas

For variety, use one of the following as a baste during cooking or as a marinade before cooking.

Italian Style
To 1 cup prepared Italian dressing, add:
   2 tablespoons grated Parmesan cheese

Mexican Style
To 1 jar (12 oz.) salsa, add:
   2 tablespoons tomato catsup

Russian Style
To 1 cup prepared Russian dressing, add:
   1 tablespoon dried parsley flakes
   1 tablespoon finely chopped onion
   ⅛ teaspoon celery seed

Sweet & Sour
To 1 cup prepared sweet & sour sauce, add:
   ¼ cup drained, crushed pineapple
   1 tablespoon sliced green onion

Orange Blossom
To 1 jar (10 oz.) orange marmalade, add:
   1 tablespoon soy sauce
   1 tablespoon sliced green onions
   ¼ teaspoon ground ginger

Each recipe coats 2½ to 3 pounds chicken.

Orange-glazed Chicken ▲

⅓ cup orange marmalade
 1 tablespoon olive or vegetable oil
 2 teaspoons white wine vinegar
½ teaspoon dried mint leaves
¼ teaspoon dried rosemary leaves, crushed
¼ teaspoon bouquet sauce
⅛ teaspoon garlic powder
2½ to 3-lb. whole broiler-fryer chicken, cut into
     8 pieces, skin removed

4 servings

1 Blend all ingredients, except the chicken, in a 2-cup measure. Microwave at 50% (Medium) for 1 to 1½ minutes, or until glaze mixture is warm. Stir.

2 Arrange chicken pieces on a roasting rack with thickest portions toward outside. Brush glaze mixture on chicken. Cover with wax paper.

3 Microwave chicken at 70% (Medium High) for 15 to 25 minutes, or until meat near the bone is no longer pink and the juices run clear, rearranging and brushing chicken pieces with glaze twice during cooking time. Let chicken stand, covered, for 3 to 5 minutes before serving.

Total Cooking Time: 16 to 26½ minutes

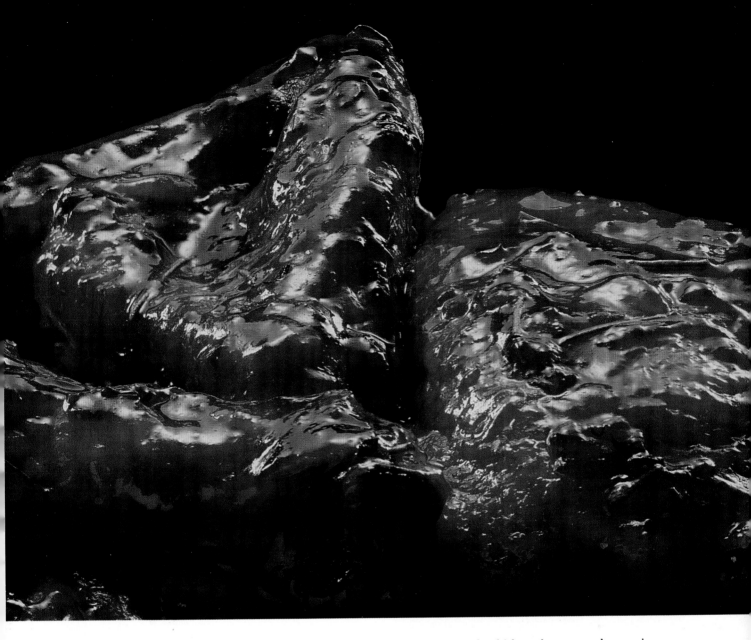

Salsa Chicken

  1 can (16 oz.) kidney beans, drained
  1 cup frozen corn
2½ to 3-lb. whole broiler-fryer chicken, cut into
     8 pieces, skin removed
  1 jar (12 oz.) salsa sauce
  3 tablespoons tomato paste
  1 teaspoon instant chicken bouillon granules
 ½ teaspoon dried oregano leaves

4 servings

1 Combine the kidney beans and corn in a 10-inch square casserole. Arrange the chicken pieces over the vegetables, with thickest portions toward outside edges of casserole.

2 Combine the remaining ingredients in a small mixing bowl. Pour mixture over the chicken; cover. Microwave at High for 3 minutes.

3 Microwave chicken at 70% (Medium High) for 25 to 32 minutes longer, or until meat near the bone is no longer pink and the juices run clear, rotating casserole 3 times during cooking. If desired, serve over hot cooked rice.

Total Cooking Time: 28 to 35 minutes

Quick Coatings for Chicken Pieces

Add flavor, variety and an attractive finish to basic chicken

Now you can duplicate the taste and texture of old-fashioned fried chicken in less time than ever before, with fewer calories, and without the old-fashioned mess.

Calorie-cutting Tip:
Remove chicken skin before microwaving. The coatings will adhere directly to the meat, and you'll avoid unwanted calories. Each of the recipes on this page will coat 2½ to 3 lbs. of chicken pieces.

How to Microwave Coated Chicken Pieces

1 Combine coating ingredients in a shallow casserole or on wax paper; set aside. Mix dip ingredients in a small bowl. Moisten chicken in dip, then roll in coating, pressing to coat. Arrange chicken pieces bone-side-down in a baking dish or on a roasting rack, with thickest portions toward outside.

Savory Cracker-coated Chicken

Coating:
1½ cups finely crushed round buttery crackers (30 to 35)
1 envelope (1¼ oz.) onion soup mix
Dip:
1 large egg, beaten
2 tablespoons milk or melted butter

Follow photo directions, below.

Total Cooking Time: 18 to 25 minutes

Coating Variations:

Herbed Coating:
Combine the following ingredients: 1½ cups herb-seasoned stuffing mix, finely crushed; ¾ teaspoon dried basil leaves; ⅛ to ¼ teaspoon garlic powder.

Fried Onion Ring Coating: (left)
Crush 2 cans (3 oz. each) fried onion rings.

Light Crumb Coating: (right)
Combine the following ingredients: ½ cup instant mashed potato flakes; ½ cup seasoned dry bread crumbs; 1 teaspoon dried parsley flakes; ½ teaspoon salt.

2 Microwave at High for 10 minutes. Rearrange chicken so less-cooked portions are toward outside edges, but do not turn pieces over. Microwave chicken at High for 8 to 15 minutes longer, or until meat near the bone is no longer pink and the juices run clear.

◄ Bran-Herb Coated Chicken

Coating:

1½ cups bran flakes cereal, finely crushed
⅓ cup cornflake crumbs
2 tablespoons grated Parmesan cheese
½ teaspoon ground marjoram
¼ teaspoon dried rosemary leaves, crushed
¼ teaspoon pepper

¼ cup butter or margarine
2½ to 3-lb. whole broiler-fryer chicken, cut into
    8 pieces, skin removed

4 servings

1 Combine the coating ingredients on a sheet of wax paper. Set aside. In a small bowl, microwave the butter at High for 1¼ to 1½ minutes, or until melted.

2 Dip the chicken pieces in the melted butter, then roll in the coating mixture, pressing lightly to coat. Arrange the chicken pieces bone-side-down on a roasting rack, with the thickest portions toward outside.

3 Microwave at High for 8 minutes; rearrange chicken pieces so less-cooked portions are toward outside (do not turn over). Microwave chicken at High for 5 to 11 minutes longer, or until meat near the bone is no longer pink and the juices run clear.

Total Cooking Time: 14¼ to 20½ minutes

Cashew-coated Chicken

Coating:

¼ cup cashews, divided
¼ cup cornflake crumbs
½ teaspoon five-spice powder (optional)
¼ teaspoon salt
    Dash pepper

1 tablespoon butter or margarine
1 large egg, beaten
4 chicken drumsticks (1 lb.) skin removed

2 servings

1 Place 2 tablespoons of the cashews in a blender container; process until fine particles form. Finely chop the remaining cashews. On wax paper, combine the processed and chopped cashews and the remaining coating ingredients. Set aside.

2 In a small bowl, microwave the butter at High for 45 seconds to 1 minute, or until melted. Blend in the egg. Dip the chicken legs in the egg mixture, then roll in the coating mixture, pressing lightly to coat. Arrange chicken on a roasting rack, with thickest portions toward outside.

3 Microwave chicken at 70% (Medium High) for 7 to 12 minutes, or until meat near the bone is no longer pink and the juices run clear, rotating rack twice during cooking time.

Total Cooking Time: 7¾ to 13 minutes

Sesame-Ginger Chicken

Marinade:

½ cup chicken broth
⅓ cup soy sauce
2 tablespoons finely chopped onion
½ teaspoon sesame oil
¼ teaspoon salt
¼ teaspoon crushed red pepper flakes
⅛ teaspoon garlic powder

4 chicken thighs (1¼ lbs.) skin removed

Coating:

½ cup crushed melba cracker rounds
⅛ teaspoon garlic powder
⅛ teaspoon ground ginger

2 tablespoons butter or margarine
1 large egg, beaten

2 to 4 servings

1 Combine all the marinade ingredients in a small bowl. Microwave at High for 1½ to 2½ minutes, or just until the mixture boils. Cool marinade slightly.

2 Place the chicken thighs in a large plastic food-storage bag; pour marinade over chicken. Secure bag, and marinate in refrigerator for at least 6 hours, turning bag occasionally.

3 Mix all coating ingredients on a sheet of wax paper. Set aside. In a small bowl, microwave the butter at High for 45 seconds to 1 minute, or until melted. Blend in the egg.

4 Drain the chicken. Dip chicken thighs in the egg mixture, then roll in the crumb mixture, pressing lightly to coat. Place the chicken on a roasting rack with thickest portions toward the outside.

5 Microwave chicken at 70% (Medium High) for 18 to 23 minutes, or until meat near the bone is no longer pink and the juices run clear, rotating rack once or twice during cooking time.

Total Cooking Time: 20¼ to 26½ minutes

Chicken in Lemon-Wine Sauce

  1 cup thinly sliced carrots
  ¾ cup thinly sliced celery
  ¼ cup sliced green onion
  1 tablespoon dried parsley flakes
  ¼ cup white wine
  1 teaspoon grated lemon peel
  ½ teaspoon bouquet garni seasoning
  ½ teaspoon salt
  ½ teaspoon instant chicken bouillon granules
  ¼ teaspoon lemon pepper seasoning
2½ to 3-lb. whole broiler-fryer chicken, cut into
    8 pieces, skin removed

4 servings

Combine all ingredients, except the chicken, in a 1-quart casserole; cover. Microwave at High for 3 to 5 minutes, or until the vegetables are tender-crisp, stirring once during cooking time. Continue with photo directions, below.

Total Cooking Time: 22 to 30 minutes

How to Microwave Chicken in Lemon-Wine Sauce

1 Arrange chicken in a shallow 2½-qt. baking dish with meatiest portions toward outside edges. Pour sauce over chicken; cover with wax paper. Microwave at High for 15 minutes, rearranging and basting pieces with sauce once during cooking time.

2 Microwave at High for 4 to 10 minutes longer, or until meat near the bone is no longer pink and the juices run clear, rearranging and basting chicken pieces 2 or 3 times during cooking.

Classic Herb Chicken ▲

2½ to 3-lb. whole broiler-fryer chicken, cut into
    8 pieces, skin removed
⅓ cup white wine
 3 tablespoons olive or vegetable oil
¾ teaspoon salt
¾ teaspoon bouquet garni seasoning
¼ teaspoon sugar
¼ teaspoon dried tarragon leaves
⅛ teaspoon dry mustard
⅛ teaspoon instant minced garlic
    Dash pepper

4 servings

1 Place chicken pieces inside a large plastic
 food-storage bag; set aside. In a 1-cup
measure, blend remaining ingredients. Pour
marinade over chicken pieces and secure the
bag. Marinate chicken in the refrigerator for at
least 6 hours.

2 Remove the chicken from marinade. Arrange
 chicken pieces on a roasting rack, with thickest
portions toward outside. Cover with wax paper.
Microwave chicken at High for 13 to 19 minutes,
or until meat near the bone is no longer pink
and the juices run clear, rotating rack once or
twice during cooking time.

Total Cooking Time: 13 to 19 minutes

Speedy Chicken Stew

 1 or 2 tablespoons olive or vegetable oil
 1 large onion, chopped
½ cup chopped celery
½ cup chopped green pepper
2½ to 3-lb. whole broiler-fryer chicken, cut into
    8 pieces
 6 tablespoons all-purpose flour, divided
1¾ cups water, divided
 2 teaspoons dried parsley flakes
 1 teaspoon salt
¼ teaspoon pepper
¼ teaspoon dried rosemary leaves
 1 teaspoon instant chicken bouillon granules

4 to 6 servings

1 Combine the oil and vegetables in a 3-quart
 casserole. Cover. Microwave at High for 4 to
6½ minutes, or until vegetables are tender,
stirring once during cooking time.

2 Combine chicken pieces and 4 tablespoons of
 the flour in a large plastic food-storage bag.
Shake to coat. Add chicken to casserole and
sprinkle with the flour remaining in bag. Stir
in 1½ cups of the water, the seasonings and
bouillon. Cover.

3 Microwave chicken at High for 25 to 35
 minutes, or until meat near the bone is no
longer pink and the juices run clear, stirring
once during cooking time. Skim fat from broth.

4 Combine the remaining water and flour; stir
 into stew. Re-cover. Microwave at High for 3½
to 5½ minutes, or until the mixture thickens. Stir
before serving.

Total Cooking Time: 32½ to 47 minutes

Chicken & Rice Casserole

1¼ cups hot tap water
  1 can (10¾ oz.) condensed cream of
      mushroom soup
  1 cup uncooked long-grain rice
  ½ cup chopped celery
  ½ cup chopped onion
  1 envelope (2 oz.) chicken noodle soup mix
2½ to 3-lb. whole broiler-fryer chicken, cut into
      8 pieces, skin removed
  1 tablespoon butter or margarine
  1 teaspoon bouquet sauce

4 servings

1 In a 3-quart casserole, combine the water, mushroom soup, rice, celery, onion and soup mix. Cover. Microwave at High for 5 minutes.

2 Microwave at 50% (Medium) for 20 to 28 minutes longer, or until the rice is almost tender; stir. Arrange chicken on top of the rice.

3 In a small bowl, microwave the butter at High for 45 seconds to 1 minute, or until melted. Add the bouquet sauce. Brush chicken with butter mixture. Cover chicken with wax paper.

4 Microwave at High for 14 to 18 minutes, or until meat near the bone is no longer pink and the rice is tender, rearranging the chicken pieces once or twice during cooking time. Let stand for 5 minutes before serving.

Total Cooking Time: 39¾ to 52 minutes

Coq Au Vin

1 medium onion, thinly sliced, separated
    into rings
⅛ teaspoon instant minced garlic
4 slices bacon, cut into 1-inch pieces
¼ cup all-purpose flour
¾ cup hot tap water
½ cup white wine
2 cups sliced fresh mushrooms
2 teaspoons dried parsley flakes
½ teaspoon salt
¼ teaspoon dried tarragon leaves
⅛ teaspoon pepper
1 small bay leaf (optional)
2½ to 3-lb. whole broiler-fryer chicken, cut into
    8 pieces, skin removed

4 to 6 servings

1 Combine the onion and garlic in a small
bowl; cover. Microwave at High for 1½ to 3
minutes, or until onion is tender-crisp. Set aside.

2 In a 3-quart casserole, microwave the bacon
at High for 4 to 6 minutes, or until crisp,
stirring once or twice during cooking time.
Drain, leaving 1 tablespoon of bacon drippings
in the casserole.

3 Stir the flour into bacon drippings; blend in
the water and wine. Stir in the onion mixture,
mushrooms, parsley, salt, tarragon, pepper and
bay leaf. Add the chicken pieces. Cover.

4 Microwave the chicken at High for 19 to 25
minutes, or until meat near the bone is no
longer pink and the juices run clear; turning over
and rearranging chicken pieces once, and stirring
sauce twice, during cooking time.

Total Cooking Time: 24½ to 34 minutes

Chicken Breasts

Chicken Breasts

Lean and nutritious, quick and delicious

Chicken breast meat is in a class by itself when placed at the center of any meal menu. Bone-in chicken breasts cost considerably less per pound than most lean meats, and yet contain as much protein as prime beef. With the skin removed, as many microwave recipes direct, chicken breast meat is very low in calories.

Microwave at High:	Time:
2 boneless or bone-in breast halves (5 to 8 oz. each)	4-8 minutes
4 boneless or bone-in breast halves (5 to 8 oz. each)	8-16 minutes

Arrange on microwave roasting rack with meaty portions toward outside.

How to Bone a Half Chicken Breast

1 Cut against breastbone to loosen meat. While angling the sharp edge of the knife toward the bone, cut against the ribs, pulling the meat away as you cut.

2 Remove wing. Scrape and pull out the tendon on the under-side of meat. Check with fingers for pieces of the wishbone which may remain.

Citrus Marinated Chicken ➤

¼ cup lemon juice
1 tablespoon soy sauce
1 tablespoon packed brown sugar
1 tablespoon vegetable oil
1 teaspoon grated orange peel
⅛ teaspoon garlic powder
2 whole bone-in chicken breasts (1½ to 2 lbs.)
   split into 4 breast halves, skin removed
4 orange slices

4 servings

1 In a 2-cup measure, combine the lemon juice, soy sauce, brown sugar, oil, orange peel and garlic powder. Microwave at High for 1 to 2 minutes, or until mixture is hot, stirring once during cooking time.

2 Place the chicken in a large plastic food-storage bag. Pour the lemon juice mixture over the chicken. Close bag and refrigerate for 1 to 2 hours. Arrange breast halves bone-side-up on a roasting rack with meatiest portions toward outside; cover with wax paper. Microwave at High for 5 minutes. Turn breasts over; top with orange slices. Re-cover.

3 Microwave chicken at High for 10 to 15 minutes longer, or until meat near the bone is no longer pink and the juices run clear, rotating the rack once during cooking time. If desired, garnish with fresh snipped parsley.

Total Cooking Time: 16 to 22 minutes

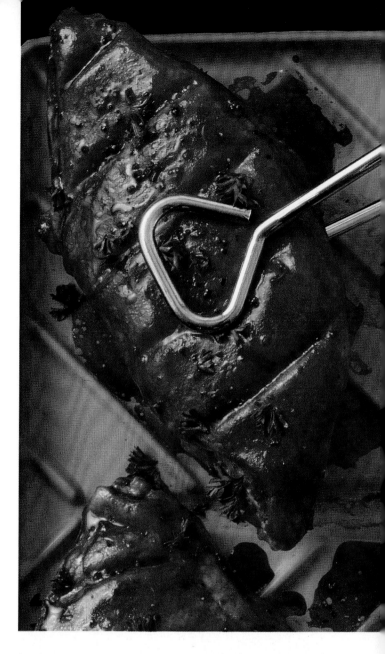

Lemon-seasoned Chicken Breasts

1 tablespoon water
1 tablespoon lemon juice
1 teaspoon lemon pepper seasoning
½ teaspoon bouquet sauce
½ teaspoon salt
2 whole bone-in chicken breasts (1½ to 2 lbs.)
   split into 4 breast halves, skin removed
1 to 2 teaspoons dried parsley flakes (optional)

4 servings

1 Combine all ingredients, except the chicken and parsley in a small dish. Arrange chicken breasts bone-side-up on a roasting rack, with meatiest portions toward outside. Brush chicken with half of the seasoning mixture. Cover with wax paper.

2 Microwave chicken at High for 5 minutes. Turn pieces over and brush with the remaining seasoning mixture. Re-cover.

3 Microwave chicken at High for 10 to 15 minutes, or until meat near the bone is no longer pink and the juices run clear, rotating the rack once during cooking time. Sprinkle with parsley before serving.

Total Cooking Time: 15 to 20 minutes

Raspberry-Lemon Sauced Chicken

2 whole bone-in chicken breasts (1½ to 2 lbs.)
   split into 4 breast halves, skin removed
   Seasoned salt

Sauce:

⅓ cup raspberry preserves
1 tablespoon butter or margarine
1 tablespoon lemon juice
4 thin lemon slices (optional)

4 servings

1 Sprinkle chicken breast halves lightly with seasoned salt. Arrange chicken bone-side-up on a roasting rack, with meaty portions toward outside. Cover with wax paper. Microwave the chicken at High for 5 minutes.

2 Turn breasts over. Re-cover; microwave at High for 10 to 15 minutes longer, or until meat near the bone is no longer pink and the juices run clear, rotating rack once or twice during cooking time. Let stand while preparing sauce.

3 Place sauce ingredients in a small bowl. Microwave at High for 30 seconds to 1 minute, or until the butter is melted and the sauce can be stirred smooth. Spoon sauce over chicken breasts; garnish with lemon slices.

Total Cooking Time: 15½ to 21 minutes

Cranberry-Orange ▲ Glazed Chicken

¼ cup orange juice
1 cup whole berry cranberry sauce
1 teaspoon cornstarch
2 whole bone-in chicken breasts (1½ to 2 lbs.)
   split into 4 breast halves, skin removed

4 servings

1 Blend all ingredients, except the chicken, in a 2-cup measure. Microwave at High for 3 to 6 minutes, or until glaze mixture is clear and thickened, stirring once or twice during cooking time. Set aside.

2 Arrange chicken bone-side-up on a roasting rack, with meatiest portions toward outside. Cover with wax paper. Microwave at High for 5 minutes. Turn the breasts over; brush with the glaze. Re-cover.

3 Microwave the chicken at High for 10 to 15 minutes longer, or until meat near the bone is no longer pink, rotating the rack once or twice during cooking time. Let stand for 5 minutes; serve with remaining glaze. (If necessary, micro-wave the glaze at High for 1 to 3 minutes, or until reheated.)

Total Cooking Time: 18 to 26 minutes

Cinnamon-Orange Spiced Chicken

2 whole bone-in chicken breasts (1½ to 2 lbs.)
   split into 4 breast halves, skin removed

Marinade:
¼ cup orange juice
2 tablespoons vermouth or water
1 teaspoon grated orange peel
1 teaspoon Worcestershire sauce
1 teaspoon onion powder
½ teaspoon ground cinnamon
¼ teaspoon ground allspice
   Dash cayenne (optional)
1 bay leaf (optional)
4 orange slices

4 servings

1 Place breast halves in a large plastic food-storage bag. Set aside. In a 1-cup measure, blend all marinade ingredients, except the bay leaf. Pour marinade over chicken; add the bay leaf. Cover. Marinate chicken in refrigerator for at least 4 hours, turning chicken over once.

2 Remove chicken from the marinade. Arrange breast halves bone-side-up on a roasting rack, with meaty portions toward outside. Cover with wax paper. Microwave chicken at High for 5 minutes. Turn breasts over. Re-cover.

3 Microwave the chicken at High for 10 to 15 minutes longer, or until meat near the bone is no longer pink and the juices run clear, rotating the rack twice during cooking time. Remove bay leaf and top with orange slices to serve.

Total Cooking Time: 15 to 20 minutes

Nutrition Tip:
Poultry is an excellent source of low-calorie, low-cholesterol protein. Reduce calories even further by removing the skin from chicken — that's where most excess fat is located. Micro-waved chicken will stay moist, even without the skin.

Mexican Chicken

1 tablespoon olive or vegetable oil
1 medium green pepper, thinly sliced
1 medium onion, thinly sliced
8 oz. fresh mushrooms, sliced
1 can (4 oz.) chopped green chilies, drained
2 whole bone-in chicken breasts (1½ to 2 lbs.)
    split into 4 breast halves, skin removed
¼ teaspoon dried basil leaves
¼ teaspoon dried oregano leaves
⅛ teaspoon garlic powder
1 can (16 oz.) tomato sauce

4 servings

1 In a 9-inch square baking dish, combine the oil, green pepper, onion, mushrooms and chilies. Cover dish with wax paper. Microwave at High for 4 to 8 minutes, or until vegetables are tender-crisp, stirring once during cooking time.

2 Arrange chicken breasts bone-side-up over vegetables, with meatiest portions toward outside edges of dish. Combine the spices and tomato sauce; pour tomato mixture over the chicken. Re-cover.

3 Microwave chicken at High for 15 to 20 minutes, or until meat near the bone is no longer pink, turning breasts over once, and rotating dish 2 or 3 times during cooking.

Total Cooking Time: 19 to 28 minutes

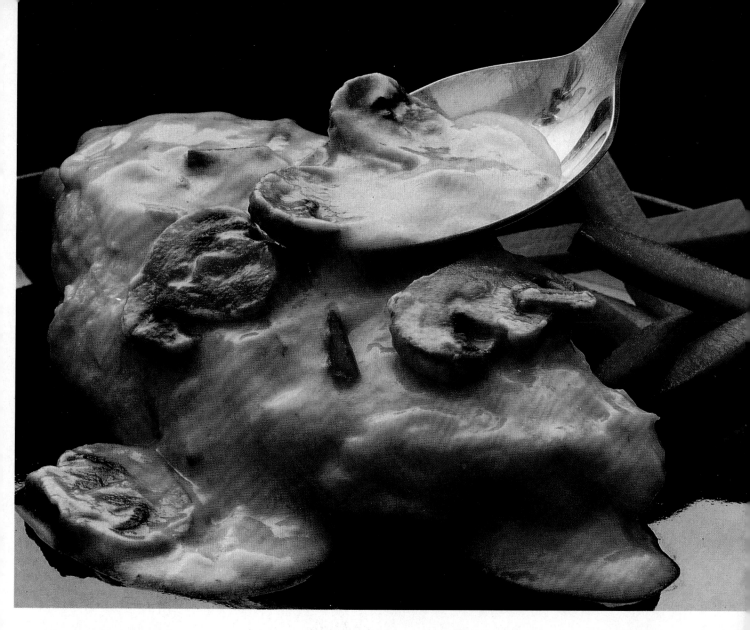

Chicken Breasts in Mushroom Sauce

8 oz. fresh mushrooms, sliced
¼ cup sliced green onions
1 tablespoon butter or margarine
2 tablespoons all-purpose flour
½ cup plain yogurt
¼ cup water
2 tablespoons dry sherry
1 teaspoon instant chicken bouillon granules
½ teaspoon salt
   Dash pepper
2 whole boneless chicken breasts (1¼ to 1½ lbs.) cut into halves, skin removed

4 servings

1 In a 1-quart casserole, combine the mushrooms, onions and butter. Cover. Microwave at High for 3 to 5 minutes, or until the mushrooms are tender. Stir in flour, then mix in remaining ingredients, except chicken.

2 Arrange the chicken pieces in a 9-inch square baking dish. Pour the sauce over the chicken, then cover the dish with wax paper.

3 Microwave at 50% (Medium) for 18 to 24 minutes, or until the sauce thickens and the chicken is no longer pink, turning and rearranging breasts, and stirring the sauce, twice during cooking time. Let chicken stand for 3 to 5 minutes; serve covered with sauce.

Total Cooking Time: 21 to 29 minutes

Sunday Chicken Bake

2 whole boneless chicken breasts (1¼ to
    1½ lbs.) cut into halves, skin removed
8 oz. fresh mushrooms, sliced
1 can (10¾ oz.) condensed cream of
    mushroom soup
⅔ cup sour cream
½ cup milk
1 tablespoon dried parsley flakes
2 cups hot cooked rice

4 servings

Follow photo directions, below.

Total Cooking Time: 28 to 33 minutes

How to Microwave Sunday Chicken Bake

1 Arrange chicken breast halves in a 9-inch square baking dish.

2 Combine the remaining ingredients, except the rice, in a small bowl; mix well. Pour mixture over chicken. Cover dish with plastic wrap.

3 Microwave at 50% (Medium) for 15 minutes. Turn chicken over, and spoon some of the sauce over the breast halves; re-cover.

4 Microwave chicken at 50% (Medium) for 13 to 18 minutes longer, or until the meat is no longer pink. Let chicken stand for 5 minutes. Serve over hot cooked rice.

Chicken & Pea Pods ►

¼ cup soy sauce
1 tablespoon cornstarch
2 teaspoons peeled grated gingerroot (or
   1 teaspoon ground ginger)
3 whole boneless chicken breasts (2 to 2¼
   lbs.) cut into ¼-inch strips, skin removed
2 pkgs. (6 oz. each) frozen pea pods
¾ cup cashews or almonds

4 to 6 servings

1 Blend the soy sauce, cornstarch and ginger-root in a 2-quart casserole. Microwave at High for 1½ minutes. Add the chicken strips; cover.

2 Microwave at High for 4 minutes; stir. Add peapods. Re-cover.

3 Microwave at High for 7 to 14 minutes, or until the chicken is no longer pink and the peapods are tender-crisp, stirring 2 or 3 times during cooking. Stir in the cashews. If desired, serve with additional soy sauce.

Total Cooking Time: 12½ to 19½ minutes

Chicken & Broccoli ▲

Marinade:

⅓ cup white wine or water
3 tablespoons soy sauce
1 tablespoon cornstarch
1 teaspoon instant chicken bouillon granules
½ teaspoon sugar
⅛ teaspoon garlic powder
⅛ teaspoon crushed red pepper flakes
   (optional)
2 whole boneless chicken breasts (1¼ to 1½
   lbs.) cut into ¼-inch strips, skin removed
3 cups fresh broccoli flowerets
1½ cups sliced fresh mushrooms
3 green onions, sliced

4 to 6 servings

1 Blend all the marinade ingredients in a 2-quart casserole. Add the strips of chicken; stir to coat. Marinate for 15 minutes at room temperature.

2 Stir in the broccoli. Cover. Microwave at High for 6 to 9 minutes, or until the chicken is still slightly pink, stirring once or twice during cooking time. Stir in the mushrooms and green onions; re-cover.

3 Microwave at High for 3 to 6 minutes, or until the broccoli is tender-crisp and chicken is no longer pink, stirring once or twice during cooking time. If desired, serve over hot cooked rice.

Total Cooking Time: 9 to 15 minutes

Oriental Chicken
with Peanut Sauce

Sauce:

- 3 tablespoons soy sauce
- 2 tablespoons lemon juice
- 1 teaspoon honey
- 1/8 teaspoon instant minced garlic
- 1/2 teaspoon peeled, grated gingerroot (or 1/4 teaspoon ground ginger)
- 1/4 teaspoon ground coriander (optional)
- 1/8 teaspoon crushed red pepper flakes
- 1/8 teaspoon sesame oil (optional)
- 3 tablespoons dry-roasted peanuts

- 1 whole boneless chicken breast (10 to 12 oz.) cut into 1/2-inch strips, skin removed
- 1/4 cup sliced green onions
- 1/2 lb. fresh spinach, torn into bite-size pieces
- 1 pkg. (3 3/4 oz.) cellophane noodles, prepared as directed on pkg.
- 1/4 cup shredded carrot

4 servings

Follow photo directions, right.

Total Cooking Time: 6 to 9 1/2 minutes

How to Microwave
Oriental Chicken with Peanut Sauce

1 Combine all sauce ingredients, except the peanuts, in a 2-cup measure. Set aside. Process the peanuts in a food processor or blender until fine particles form. Set aside.

Arroz Con Pollo ➤

2 whole boneless chicken breasts (1¼ to 1½ lbs.) cut into thin strips, skin removed
1½ cups uncooked instant rice
⅔ cup water
1 medium tomato, seeded and chopped
1 small onion, finely chopped
⅓ cup chopped green pepper
½ teaspoon salt
¼ teaspoon pepper
⅛ teaspoon ground saffron (or ¼ teaspoon ground tumeric)
⅛ teaspoon instant minced garlic
1 bay leaf (optional)

4 servings

Combine all ingredients in a 2-quart casserole; mix well. Cover. Microwave at High for 8 to 14 minutes, or until the chicken is no longer pink and the rice is tender, stirring 2 or 3 times during cooking.

Total Cooking Time: 8 to 14 minutes

2 Combine the chicken strips and onions in a 2-quart casserole. Cover. Microwave at High for 2 to 5 minutes, or until chicken is no longer pink, stirring once during cooking time. Add spinach; re-cover. Microwave at High for 2 to 2½ minutes longer, or until the spinach wilts. Stir.

3 Drain the cooking liquid from casserole into the reserved sauce mixture. Microwave sauce at High for 2 minutes to blend flavors. Stir in peanuts. Serve chicken-and-spinach mixture over cooked noodles; pour peanut sauce over the chicken, then sprinkle with shredded carrot.

Chicken Imperial

2 tablespoons butter or margarine
8 oz. fresh mushrooms, sliced
¼ cup chopped onion
2 whole bone-in chicken breasts (1½ to 2 lbs.)
   split into 4 breast halves, skin removed
2 tablespoons all-purpose flour
¼ cup white wine
1 cup whipping cream
½ teaspoon salt
⅛ teaspoon pepper

4 servings

1 Combine the butter, mushrooms and onion in a 9-inch square baking dish. Cover with wax paper. Microwave at High for 3 to 5 minutes, or until the vegetables are tender.

2 Arrange chicken breast halves bone-side-up over vegetables, with meaty portions toward the outside edges of dish. Re-cover. Microwave at High for 5 minutes, rotating dish once during cooking time.

3 In a 2-cup measure, blend the flour and wine, then stir in the cream, salt and pepper. Remove the chicken from the baking dish, and stir the cream mixture into the vegetables. Return chicken to baking dish, and spoon the vegetable-cream mixture over the chicken. Re-cover.

4 Microwave chicken at 50% (Medium) for 11 to 20 minutes, or until meat near bone is no longer pink, rotating the dish 2 or 3 times during cooking.

Total Cooking Time: 19 to 30 minutes

Crab-stuffed Chicken Breasts ➤

Crab Stuffing:

- 1 can (6 oz.) crab meat, drained and rinsed, cartilage removed
- ¼ cup sliced green onion
- 1 large egg
- 1 tablespoon dried parsley flakes
- 2 teaspoons lemon juice
- ¼ teaspoon pepper
- 2 whole boneless chicken breasts (1¼ to 1½ lbs.) cut into halves, skin removed
- 1 large egg, beaten
- ⅓ cup seasoned dry bread crumbs

4 servings

1 Combine all crab stuffing ingredients in a small bowl; mix well. Set aside. Pound each chicken breast half to a ¼-inch thickness.

2 Spread ¼ of the stuffing mixture evenly over each breast half. Roll up each breast half, tucking in sides to enclose the filling. Secure each roll with wooden picks.

3 Place the beaten egg in a shallow dish. Place the bread crumbs on a sheet of wax paper. Dip each chicken roll in egg; then roll in the bread crumbs, pressing lightly to coat.

4 Arrange the chicken rolls seam-side-down in a 9-inch square baking dish. Cover with wax paper. Microwave at High for 8 to 12 minutes, or until chicken on inside of roll is no longer pink, rearranging once during cooking time. Let stand for 3 minutes before serving.

Total Cooking Time: 8 to 12 minutes

Tarragon Chicken

- ¼ cup butter or margarine
- ¼ cup white wine
- 1 tablespoon dried parsley flakes
- 1 teaspoon instant chicken bouillon granules
- ½ teaspoon dried tarragon leaves
- ½ teaspoon salt
- ⅛ teaspoon instant minced garlic
- 2 whole bone-in chicken breasts (1½ to 2 lbs.) split into 4 breast halves, skin removed
- 4 thin lemon slices (optional)

4 servings

1 In a 9-inch square baking dish, microwave butter at High for 1¼ to 1½ minutes, or until melted. Add the wine, parsley, bouillon, tarragon, salt and garlic.

2 Dip both sides of each breast half in the butter mixture. Arrange breasts bone-side-up in the baking dish, with meaty portions toward outside edges. Cover with wax paper.

3 Microwave chicken at High for 15 to 20 minutes, or until meat near the bone is no longer pink and the juices run clear, turning chicken over after the first 5 minutes and rotating dish 2 or 3 times during cooking. Serve chicken garnished with lemon slices.

Total Cooking Time: 16¼ to 21½ minutes

Whole Chicken

Whole Chicken

*Golden brown, juicy and tender —
in less than 30 minutes*

A whole chicken turns a light golden brown during microwaving, and for a richer color you can brush the chicken with a glaze, or use a bouquet sauce mixture. Dilute bouquet sauce with butter and rub into skin for better browning.

Whole Chicken (2½-3 lb.)	Power:	Time:
Defrost	30% (Med. Low)	5-9 min./lb.
Cook	High	5-8 min./lb.

How to Microwave a Whole Chicken

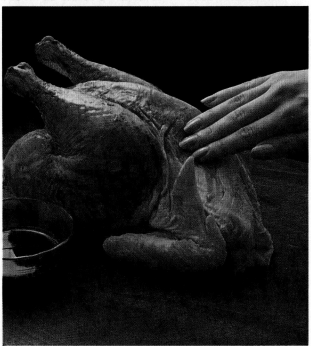

1 Thoroughly dry a 2½ to 3-lb. whole broiler-fryer chicken. Blend equal parts of bouquet sauce and melted butter; rub mixture onto skin.

2 Place chicken breast-side-down in a baking dish. Microwave at High for 10 minutes.

3 Turn chicken breast-side-up. Microwave for 8 to 15 minutes longer, or until the legs move freely at joints, meat near the bone is no longer pink and the juices run clear. Let chicken stand 10 minutes before carving.

Vegetable-stuffed Chicken

1½ cups cubed eggplant (½-inch cubes)
  1 medium green pepper, cut into ¾-inch
      chunks
  1 medium tomato, seeded and chopped
  ⅓ cup chopped onion
  ¼ teaspoon garlic powder
  1 tablespoon olive or vegetable oil
  ½ teaspoon dried basil leaves
2½ to 3-lb. whole broiler-fryer chicken
  1 tablespoon butter or margarine
  1 teaspoon bouquet sauce

4 servings

1 In a 1-quart casserole, combine the eggplant, green pepper, tomato, onion, garlic powder, oil and basil. Cover. Microwave at High for 4 to 8 minutes, or until the vegetables are tender-crisp, stirring once during cooking time.

2 Spoon the stuffing into cavity of the chicken. Secure legs together with string. Place chicken breast-side-down on a roasting rack.

3 In a small bowl, microwave the butter at High for 45 seconds to 1 minute, or until melted. Stir in the bouquet sauce. Brush chicken with half of the sauce mixture.

4 Microwave chicken at High for 28 to 34 minutes, or until meat near the bone is no longer pink and the juices run clear, turning breast-side up and brushing with remaining bouquet sauce mixture after first 10 minutes of cooking time. Let chicken stand for 10 minutes before serving.

Total Cooking Time: 32¾ to 43 minutes

Preparation Tip:
When preparing stuffed whole poultry, always use a pre-cooked hot stuffing mixture. Secure legs together with string, if desired. Microwave as directed, until internal temperature of the stuffing mixture is at least 145°F and meaty portion of thigh registers 185°F.

Herb-roasted Chicken

½ teaspoon grated lemon peel
½ teaspoon dried oregano leaves
¼ teaspoon dried crushed sage leaves
¼ teaspoon dried marjoram leaves
¼ teaspoon pepper, divided
⅛ teaspoon instant minced garlic

2½ to 3-lb. whole broiler-fryer chicken
1 small onion, sliced
1 bay leaf
½ teaspoon dried parsley flakes

4 servings

Follow photo directions, below.

Total Cooking Time: 18 to 25 minutes

How to Microwave Herb-roasted Chicken

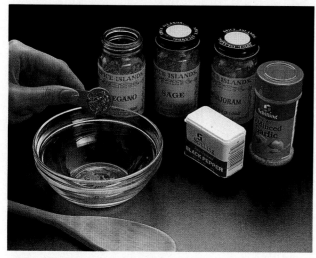

1 In a small bowl, mix lemon peel, oregano, sage, marjoram, ⅛ teaspoon of the pepper, and the garlic.

2 Loosen skin gently and lift from breast and legs of chicken. Rub herb mixture under skin; replace skin. Place onion and bay leaf in cavity of chicken.

3 Secure legs together with string. In a small bowl, mix parsley and remaining pepper. Rub onto chicken skin. Place chicken breast-side-up on roasting rack.

4 Microwave at High for 18 to 25 minutes, or until the meat near the bone is no longer pink and the juices run clear. Let stand, covered, for 10 minutes before carving.

Pineapple Glazed Chicken

½ cup pineapple preserves
⅓ cup prepared Russian salad dressing
2½ to 3-lb. whole broiler-fryer chicken

4 servings

1 Mix the pineapple preserves and Russian dressing in a small bowl. Secure legs of chicken together with string. Place the chicken breast-side-down on a roasting rack. Brush with half of the pineapple mixture.

2 Microwave the chicken at High for 20 to 28 minutes, or until meat near the bone is no longer pink and the juices run clear, turning breast-side up and brushing with remaining sauce after first 10 minutes of cooking time. Let chicken stand for 10 minutes before carving.

Total Cooking Time: 20 to 28 minutes

◄ Soy-Garlic Glazed Chicken

2 teaspoons soy sauce
1 tablespoon white wine
  Water
1 teaspoon cornstarch
⅛ teaspoon garlic powder
2½ to 3-lb. whole broiler-fryer chicken

4 servings

1 Combine soy sauce and wine in a 1-cup measure. Add enough water to equal ½ cup. Blend in cornstarch and garlic powder. Micro-wave at High for 1 to 3 minutes, or until sauce is clear and thickened, stirring once during cooking time.

2 Secure legs of chicken together with string. Place chicken breast-side-down on a roasting rack. Brush with half the sauce mixture.

3 Microwave chicken at High for 18 to 25 minutes, or until meat near the bone is no longer pink and the juices run clear, turning breast-side up and brushing with remaining sauce after first 10 minutes of cooking time. Let stand for 10 minutes before carving.

Total Cooking Time: 19 to 28 minutes

Roast Chicken with Noodles

1 pkg. (10 oz.) frozen mixed vegetables
2½ to 3-lb. whole broiler-fryer chicken
1 tablespoon butter or margarine
1 teaspoon bouquet sauce
2 cups uncooked egg noodles, prepared as
   directed on pkg.
1 can (10¾ oz.) condensed cream of
   celery soup
1 teaspoon instant chicken bouillon granules
¼ teaspoon dry mustard
¼ teaspoon salt
   Dash pepper

4 servings

1 Unwrap mixed vegetables and place on plate.
Microwave at High for 4 to 6 minutes, or until
defrosted, turning over and breaking apart once
during cooking time. Set aside. Secure legs of
chicken together with string. Place chicken
breast-side-down in a 3-quart deep casserole.

2 In a small bowl, microwave the butter at High
for 45 seconds to 1 minute, or until melted.
Add the bouquet sauce. Brush chicken with half
of the butter mixture.

3 Microwave chicken at High for 18 to 23
minutes, or until meat near the bone is no
longer pink and the juices run clear, turning
breast-side up and brushing with remaining
butter mixture after first 10 minutes of cooking
time. Drain.

4 In a medium bowl, combine the vegetables,
cooked noodles, the soup, bouillon, mustard,
salt and pepper. Spoon noodle mixture evenly
around chicken. Cover. Microwave mixture at
High for 4 to 8 minutes, or until heated, stirring
once during cooking time.

Total Cooking Time: 26¾ to 38 minutes

Browning Tip:
Browning sauce mixtures can be applied to
chicken in varying degrees to achieve the
color you prefer. If the sauce beads up or
streaks, try patting the skin dry and rubbing
the sauce in with your fingers.

Stuffed Chicken Italiano

Stuffing:

   3 tablespoons butter or margarine
 ⅔ cup seasoned dry bread crumbs
   3 tablespoons grated Parmesan or Romano
      cheese
 ½ teaspoon Italian seasoning

2½ to 3-lb. whole broiler-fryer chicken
   1 can (16 oz.) whole tomatoes, drained and
      cut up

1¾ cups chicken broth
   1 medium onion, cut into 8 wedges
 ⅓ cup white wine
 ½ teaspoon salt

                                      4 servings

In a medium bowl, microwave the butter at High for 45 seconds to 1 minute, or until melted. Stir in bread crumbs, cheese and Italian seasoning. Continue with photo directions, right.

Total Cooking Time: 20¾ to 36 minutes

How to Microwave Stuffed Chicken Italiano

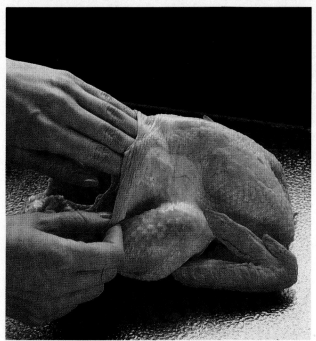

1 Loosen chicken skin and gently lift away from the breast of the chicken.

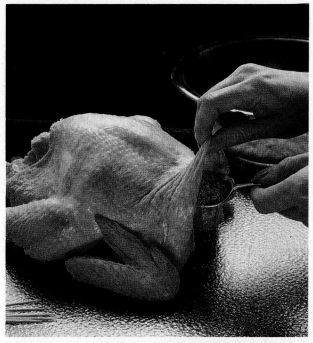

2 Stuff crumb mixture under the skin. Replace skin and secure with wooden picks.

3 Secure legs together with string. Place chicken breast-side-up in a 3-quart deep casserole. Add the remaining ingredients.

4 Microwave at High for 20 to 35 minutes, or until meat near bone is no longer pink and juices run clear, rotating casserole and basting with broth several times during cooking. Let stand for 10 minutes before carving.

Soups & Stews

Light & satisfying, quick & complete

Microwaved soups and stews using chicken are among the most nutritious and economical meals to be found. Whether you use leftovers from a roast bird or canned convenience chicken, nothing goes to waste. Try one of the following recipes for a hearty, complete fast-lunch, or add elegance to a more sophisticated evening dinner.

Chicken Stew

- 3 tablespoons butter or margarine
- ½ cup chopped onion
- ½ cup thinly sliced carrot
- ¼ cup all-purpose flour
- 2 cups water
- 2 cups coarsely shredded cabbage
- 1 can (10½ oz.) condensed chicken and rice soup
- 1 to 1½ cups cut-up cooked chicken
- ½ cup thin strips yellow squash
- ¼ cup frozen peas
- ¾ teaspoon salt
- ¼ teaspoon dried rosemary leaves, crushed
- ⅛ teaspoon pepper

4 to 6 servings

1 Combine the butter, onion and carrot in a 2-quart casserole. Cover. Microwave at High for 4 to 6 minutes, or until the carrot is tender-crisp, stirring once during cooking time.

2 Stir in flour; blend in the water and remaining ingredients. Re-cover. Microwave at High for 15 to 23 minutes, or until the stew thickens slightly and the cabbage is tender, stirring 3 or 4 times during cooking.

Total Cooking Time: 19 to 29 minutes

Old-fashioned Chicken-Noodle Soup

2½ to 3-lb. whole broiler-fryer chicken, cut into
     8 pieces, skin removed
5½ cups hot tap water, divided
  2 stalks celery, thinly sliced
  2 medium carrots, thinly sliced
  1 teaspoon salt
  ½ teaspoon dried basil leaves
  ¼ teaspoon dried marjoram leaves
  ¼ teaspoon pepper
  ½ cup uncooked thin egg noodles

8 servings

1 In a 3-quart casserole, combine the chicken, 3½ cups of the hot water, celery, carrots, salt, basil, marjoram and pepper. Cover.

2 Microwave at High for 30 to 40 minutes, or until meat near the bone is no longer pink, stirring to rearrange the pieces twice during cooking time.

3 Remove the chicken from the bones; discard bones. Dice meat and return to the casserole. Add remaining hot water and noodles. Cover.

4 Microwave at High for 15 to 20 minutes, or until the mixture is very hot and the noodles are tender, stirring 2 or 3 times during cooking.

Total Cooking Time: 45 to 60 minutes

Cooking Tip:
For variety, try preparing Old-fashioned Chicken-Noodle Soup with dried summer savory leaves instead of dried basil and marjoram leaves. Sprinkle each serving with grated Parmesan cheese, and serve with crisp garlic toasts.

Chicken Chili

½ cup chopped onion
½ cup chopped green pepper
⅛ teaspoon instant minced garlic
 1 can (16 oz.) kidney beans, rinsed and
    drained
 1 can (16 oz.) whole tomatoes
 1 can (8 oz.) tomato sauce
 1 can (8 oz.) corn, drained
 1 cup cut-up cooked chicken
 2 tablespoons red wine vinegar
 2 tablespoons Worcestershire sauce
 1 tablespoon packed brown sugar
 1 to 2 teaspoons chili powder

6 servings

1 Combine the onion, green pepper and garlic in a 2-quart casserole. Cover. Microwave at High for 2 to 4 minutes, or until the vegetables are tender-crisp.

2 Add the remaining ingredients, stirring to break apart tomatoes. Cover. Microwave at 70% (Medium High) for 25 to 30 minutes, or until the flavors are blended and the chili is hot, stirring twice during cooking time.

Total Cooking Time: 27 to 34 minutes

Chicken-Okra Gumbo

2½ to 3-lb. whole broiler-fryer chicken, cut into
    8 pieces
½ teaspoon dried thyme leaves
¼ teaspoon dried basil leaves
⅛ teaspoon cayenne
1 bay leaf
1 cup water
⅛ teaspoon instant minced garlic
2 tablespoons vegetable oil
1 medium onion, thinly sliced
1 medium green pepper, chopped
3 tablespoons all-purpose flour
1 can (16 oz.) whole tomatoes, cut up
1 pkg. (10 oz.) frozen cut okra
1 cup cubed fully cooked ham (½-inch cubes)
1 can (6 oz.) vegetable juice cocktail
1 teaspoon salt
1 teaspoon Worcestershire sauce

4 servings

Follow photo directions, below.

Total Cooking Time: 41 to 52 minutes

How to Microwave Chicken-Okra Gumbo

1 Arrange chicken in 3-quart casserole, with meaty portions toward the outside edges. Sprinkle with thyme, basil and cayenne. Add bay leaf, water and garlic.

2 Microwave at High for 16 to 20 minutes, or until meat near the bone is no longer pink, turning chicken over once. Skim fat; strain and reserve broth. Remove chicken from bones. Dice meat. Set aside.

3 Combine the oil, onion, and green pepper in the same casserole. Cover. Microwave at High for 5 to 7 minutes, or until the onion is tender, stirring once during cooking time.

4 Stir in flour. Add reserved broth, chicken and remaining ingredients. Cover. Microwave at High for 20 to 25 minutes, or until the mixture thickens, stirring 2 or 3 times during cooking. If desired, serve over hot cooked rice.

Quick Chicken & Wild Rice Soup

⅓ cup chopped carrot
1 tablespoon butter or margarine
⅛ teaspoon dried thyme leaves
   Dash dried marjoram leaves
1 tablespoon all-purpose flour
¼ teaspoon salt
1 cup chicken broth
½ cup milk
2 egg yolks, beaten
½ cup cut-up cooked chicken
½ cup cooked wild rice

4 to 6 servings

1 In a 1½-quart casserole, combine the carrot, butter, thyme and marjoram. Cover. Microwave at High for 3 to 7 minutes, or until the carrot is tender-crisp.

2 Stir in the flour and salt. Blend in the broth, milk and egg yolks. Stir in the chicken and the wild rice.

3 Microwave at 70% (Medium High) for 6 to 9 minutes, or just until the mixture thickens and bubbles, stirring 2 or 3 times during cooking.

Total Cooking Time: 9 to 16 minutes

Savory Chicken & Rice Soup

- 3 tablespoons butter or margarine
- ⅓ cup chopped carrot
- ⅓ cup chopped celery
- 2 tablespoons sliced green onion (optional)
- 1 teaspoon dried marjoram leaves (optional)
- 3 tablespoons all-purpose flour
- 1 whole boneless chicken breast (10 to 12 oz.) cut into thin strips, skin removed
- 1¾ cups chicken broth
- 1 cup sliced fresh mushrooms
- 1 cup cooked white or brown rice
- ½ teaspoon salt
- 1 cup milk
- 2 egg yolks, beaten

4 to 6 servings

1 In a 3-quart casserole, combine the butter, carrot, celery, onion and marjoram. Cover. Microwave at High for 6 to 7 minutes, or until the vegetables are tender, stirring once or twice during cooking time.

2 Stir in the flour, chicken strips, broth, mushrooms, rice and salt. Re-cover. Microwave at High for 8 to 10 minutes, or until the mixture is thickened and the mushrooms are tender, stirring 2 or 3 times during cooking. Set aside.

3 Blend the milk and egg yolks in a small bowl. Pour milk and egg mixture slowly into the soup, stirring until blended. Re-cover.

4 Microwave at 50% (Medium) for 3 to 7 minutes, or until the chicken is no longer pink and the soup is heated through, stirring once during cooking time.

Total Cooking Time: 17 to 24 minutes

Lemony Chicken Soup

  3 tablespoons butter or margarine, divided
⅓ cup sliced almonds
  1 cup shredded carrot
  2 tablespoons sliced green onion
  1 tablespoon dried parsley flakes
  2 tablespoons all-purpose flour
3½ cups chicken broth
  3 tablespoons lemon juice
½ teaspoon salt
  3 egg yolks, beaten
  1 cup cut-up cooked chicken
  1 cup cooked rice (optional)

4 to 6 servings

1 Combine 1 tablespoon of the butter and the almonds in a 1-quart casserole. Microwave at High for 3½ to 4½ minutes, or just until the almonds begin to brown, stirring once during cooking time. Set aside.

2 In a 2-quart casserole, combine the carrots, onion, parsley and remaining butter. Cover. Microwave at High for 3 to 4 minutes, or until the carrots are tender-crisp, stirring once during cooking time.

3 Stir in the flour. Blend in the broth, lemon juice and salt. Microwave at High for 10 to 16 minutes, or until the mixture boils.

4 Whisk a small amount of the hot broth mixture into the egg yolks. Return egg yolk mixture to the hot broth, blending with a whisk. Stir in the chicken and rice.

5 Microwave at 50% (Medium) for 3 to 6 minutes, or until mixture is heated through and slightly thickened, stirring twice during cooking time. Stir in the almonds.

Total Cooking Time: 19½ to 30½ minutes

Chicken-Cheddar Soup

2½ to 3-lb. whole broiler-fryer chicken, cut into
    8 pieces, skin removed
 ½ cup water
 ⅓ cup chopped onion
 1 tablespoon butter or margarine
 ½ teaspoon ground cumin
 1 can (16 oz.) whole tomatoes, cut up
 2 tablespoons canned chopped green chilies
 2 tablespoons all-purpose flour
 2 cups finely shredded Cheddar cheese
 ½ teaspoon salt
 1 cup half-and-half

4 to 6 servings

1 Combine the chicken and water in a 3-quart
casserole. Cover. Microwave at High for 16 to
20 minutes, or until meat near the bone is no
longer pink, stirring to rearrange pieces twice
during cooking time.

2 Strain and reserve the chicken broth. Remove
chicken from the bones. Discard bones; dice
the chicken meat and set aside.

3 In the same casserole, combine the onion,
butter and cumin. Cover. Microwave at High
for 3 to 6 minutes, or until the onion is tender.
Add the reserved broth, diced chicken, tomatoes
and chilies. Stir to combine.

4 Shake flour and cheese in a large plastic food-
storage bag until cheese is coated. Stir coated
cheese into the chicken-and-tomato mixture, then
blend in remaining ingredients. Re-cover.

5 Microwave at 50% (Medium) for 15 to 20
minutes, or until the cheese is melted and the
mixture is heated through, stirring 3 or 4 times
during cooking.

Total Cooking Time: 34 to 46 minutes

Salads

*For easy menu variety,
try these fresh ideas*

Marinated Chicken & Bean Salad

1 pkg. (9 oz.) frozen artichoke hearts
1 whole boneless chicken breast (10 to 12 oz.)
   cut into 1-inch cubes, skin removed
½ cup chopped onion
⅛ teaspoon instant minced garlic
⅛ teaspoon dried thyme leaves
1 can (16 oz.) Great Northern Beans, rinsed
   and drained
⅓ cup chopped green or red pepper
1 tablespoon dried parsley flakes

Dressing:
3 tablespoons olive or vegetable oil
2 tablespoons white wine vinegar
1 teaspoon salt

4 servings

Follow photo directions, right.

Total Cooking Time: 7 to 10½ minutes

2 Add chicken, onion, garlic and thyme. Re-cover. Microwave at High for 4 to 6½ minutes, or until the chicken is no longer pink, stirring twice during cooking time. Drain. Stir in the beans, green pepper and parsley.

How to Microwave Marinated Chicken & Bean Salad

1 Unwrap artichoke hearts and place in a 2-quart casserole. Cover. Microwave at High for 3 to 4 minutes, or until defrosted, stirring to break apart once during cooking time.

3 Blend dressing ingredients in a 1-cup measure; pour over chicken mixture. Toss to coat. Cover and chill for at least 3 hours before serving.

Tropical Chicken-Melon Salad

2 slices bacon, chopped
1 whole boneless chicken breast (10 to 12 oz.)
    cut into ¾-inch cubes, skin removed
1 small onion, thinly sliced
½ teaspoon dried marjoram leaves
½ teaspoon salt
⅓ cup mayonnaise
1 pkg. (7 oz.) uncooked spaghetti, prepared as
    directed on pkg.
2 cups cubed cantaloupe (¾-inch cubes)
1 avocado, cut into ¾-inch cubes

                            4 to 6 servings

1 In a 2-quart casserole, microwave the bacon at High for 2½ to 3½ minutes, or until crisp, stirring once or twice during cooking time.

2 Remove bacon with a slotted spoon; set aside. Leave the bacon drippings in the casserole. Stir in the chicken, onion, marjoram and salt. Mix well. Cover; microwave at High for 3½ to 4 minutes, or until chicken is no longer pink, stirring 2 or 3 times during cooking.

3 Drain the cooking liquid into a small bowl, and blend in the mayonnaise and the bacon. Pour mayonnaise mixture over hot cooked spaghetti; toss to coat.

4 Add cantaloupe to the chicken mixture; serve over spaghetti. Top with avocado cubes.

Total Cooking Time: 6 to 7½ minutes

Mediterranean Chicken Salad

2½ to 3-lb. whole broiler-fryer chicken,
    quartered
1 teaspoon dried oregano leaves
½ teaspoon salt
¼ teaspoon pepper
½ cup red wine
2 cups peeled cubed eggplant (½-inch cubes)
½ cup chopped red onion
⅛ teaspoon instant minced garlic
2 medium tomatoes, seeded and chopped
⅓ cup sliced black olives

Dressing:
3 tablespoons olive or vegetable oil
2 tablespoons lemon juice
1 tablespoon snipped fresh parsley
¾ teaspoon salt
½ teaspoon dried oregano leaves
¼ teaspoon sugar
¼ teaspoon pepper

6 servings

1 Arrange the chicken in a shallow 3-quart casserole, with the meaty portions toward outside edges. Sprinkle with oregano, salt and pepper. Pour wine over chicken. Cover.

2 Microwave chicken at High for 16 to 22 minutes, or until meat near the bone is no longer pink and the juices run clear, turning chicken over once during cooking time. Reserve 2 tablespoons chicken broth.

3 Place reserved broth in a 2-quart casserole. Add the eggplant, onion and garlic; cover. Microwave at High for 5 to 7 minutes, or until the eggplant is tender, stirring once during cooking time.

4 Remove chicken from bones; discard bones. Dice chicken meat. Add the diced chicken, tomatoes and olives to the eggplant mixture. Combine all dressing ingredients in a 1-cup measure; mix well. Pour dressing over chicken and vegetables; toss to coat. Cover and chill for at least 3 hours before serving.

Total Cooking Time: 21 to 29 minutes

◄ Hot Chicken Salad

 1 medium onion, chopped
 1 medium green pepper, chopped
 2 tablespoons butter or margarine
 3 cups cubed cooked chicken
 1 cup sliced almonds
 ½ cup fresh bread cubes (½-inch cubes)
 2 teaspoons instant chicken bouillon granules
 ⅓ cup brandy or apple juice
 ⅛ teaspoon red pepper sauce
1½ cups shredded lettuce
 ¾ cup halved green grapes (optional)

6 to 8 servings

1 Combine the onion, green pepper and butter in a 3-quart casserole. Cover. Microwave at High for 3 to 5 minutes, or until vegetables are tender-crisp, stirring once during cooking time.

2 Stir in the remaining ingredients, except the lettuce and grapes. Re-cover. Microwave at High for 4 to 8 minutes, or until the mixture is hot, stirring once during cooking time. Stir in the lettuce and grapes.

Total Cooking Time: 7 to 13 minutes

Crunchy Chicken Salad

 1 cup chopped celery
 ¼ cup chopped onion
 3 eggs, hard-cooked, coarsely chopped
 2 cups cubed cooked chicken
 1 can (10¾ oz.) condensed cream of
    chicken soup
 ¼ cup slivered almonds
 1 tablespoon lemon juice
 2 teaspoons chopped pimiento (optional)
 ½ teaspoon salt
 ¼ teaspoon pepper
 1 can (1½ oz.) shoestring potatoes, divided

4 to 6 servings

1 Combine the celery and onion in a 1½-quart casserole. Cover. Microwave at High for 3 to 4 minutes, or until the vegetables are tender. Stir in the remaining ingredients, except for half of the shoestring potatoes.

2 Microwave, uncovered, at High for 3 minutes, stirring once during cooking time. Sprinkle with the remaining shoestring potatoes. Microwave at High for 2 to 5 minutes longer, or until salad is heated through.

Total Cooking Time: 8 to 12 minutes

Chicken & Spinach Salad

¾ lb. fresh spinach, torn into bite-size pieces
1 can (11 oz.) mandarin orange segments, drained
1 cup fresh bean sprouts
1 cup shredded cooked chicken
½ cup walnut halves
2 slices bacon, chopped
  Vegetable oil
3 tablespoons cider vinegar
1 teaspoon freeze-dried chives
¼ teaspoon dry mustard
  Dash pepper

6 to 8 servings

1 In a large bowl, combine the spinach, oranges, bean sprouts, chicken and walnuts. Set aside.

2 In a small bowl, microwave the bacon at High for 2½ to 3½ minutes, or until crisp, stirring once or twice during cooking time. Remove bacon with a slotted spoon. Add bacon to the chicken mixture; reserve bacon drippings. Set aside.

3 Add enough vegetable oil to the bacon drippings to equal ¼ cup. Stir in the remaining ingredients. Microwave at High for 30 to 45 seconds, or until mixture is hot. Pour dressing over the salad; toss to coat.

Total Cooking Time: 3 to 4¼ minutes

Hot Chicken Waldorf

1 can (5 oz.) chunk chicken, drained
⅔ cup chopped apple
½ cup shredded Swiss cheese
½ cup mayonnaise
2 tablespoons chopped celery
2 tablespoons sunflower nuts
1 tablespoon sliced green onion
1 teaspoon lemon juice
¼ teaspoon lemon pepper seasoning
6 frozen patty shells, prepared as directed
    on pkg.

6 servings

Combine all ingredients, except the patty shells, in a 1-quart casserole. Mix well. Microwave at High for 2½ to 4 minutes, or until the cheese melts and the mixture is hot, stirring twice during cooking time. Spoon chicken mixture into patty shells to serve.

Total Cooking Time: 2½ to 4 minutes

Variation:

Hot Chicken Waldorf Sandwiches:
Substitute 6 whole wheat hamburger buns, split, for the patty shells.

How to Microwave Hot Chicken Waldorf Sandwiches

1 Combine all ingredients, except buns, together in a small bowl.

2 Arrange bottom halves of buns on a paper-towel-lined platter. Top each with about ⅓ cup chicken mixture.

3 Microwave at High for 3 to 5 minutes, or until mixture is hot and cheese melts, rotating platter once. Top the sandwiches with remaining bun halves.

Creative Leftovers

Turn leftover chicken into delightful dinners

◄ Shredded Chicken & Cashews

⅓ cup chicken broth
1 tablespoon soy sauce
1 tablespoon white wine
1 teaspoon sugar
1 teaspoon cornstarch
½ teaspoon salt
¼ teaspoon crushed red pepper flakes
¼ teaspoon sesame oil (optional)
⅛ teaspoon instant minced garlic
2 cups shredded cooked chicken
2 teaspoons vegetable oil
1 medium carrot, cut into thin strips
½ cup sliced fresh mushrooms
½ cup sliced green onions
½ cup sliced water chestnuts
⅓ cup chopped cashews

4 to 6 servings

1 In a medium bowl, combine the broth, soy sauce, wine, sugar, cornstarch, salt, red pepper, sesame oil and garlic. Mix well. Add the chicken; stir to coat. Set aside.

2 In a 2-quart casserole, combine the vegetable oil, carrot, mushrooms, onions and water chestnuts. Cover. Microwave at High for 4 to 5½ minutes, or just until the carrot is tender-crisp, stirring once during cooking time.

3 Add the chicken mixture and cashews; stir. Re-cover. Microwave at High for 3 to 5 minutes, or until the mixture is very hot, stirring once during cooking time. If desired, serve over hot cooked rice.

Total Cooking Time: 7 to 10½ minutes

Chicken-stuffed Tomatoes ▲

4 large tomatoes
1 pkg. (9 oz.) frozen artichoke hearts
2 cups cubed cooked chicken
2 tablespoons grated Parmesan cheese
¼ teaspoon garlic powder
¼ teaspoon dried marjoram leaves
¼ teaspoon salt
⅛ teaspoon pepper
Paprika (optional)

4 servings

1 Cut a thin slice from the stem end of each tomato. Scoop out the pulp. (Pulp can be reserved and frozen for future use in sauces.)

2 Unwrap artichoke hearts and place on a plate. Microwave at High for 3 to 4 minutes, or until artichokes are defrosted, stirring to break apart once during cooking time. Drain. Chop artichokes into small pieces. Set aside.

3 In a medium bowl, combine the artichokes, chicken, Parmesan cheese, garlic powder, marjoram, salt and pepper. Spoon mixture into the tomato shells, and sprinkle with paprika.

4 Place each tomato in a custard cup or small bowl. Microwave stuffed tomatoes at High for 5 to 8 minutes, or until heated. If desired, top each tomato with a dollop of mayonnaise.

Total Cooking Time: 8 to 12 minutes

Walnut Pasta & Chicken

1 pkg. (10 oz.) frozen chopped broccoli
⅓ cup chopped onion
2 tablespoons water
⅛ teaspoon instant minced garlic
1½ cups uncooked whole wheat or egg elbow
    macaroni, prepared as directed on pkg.
2 cups cubed cooked chicken
¼ teaspoon Italian seasoning
⅛ teaspoon pepper
1 cup sour cream or plain yogurt
2 tablespoons grated Parmesan cheese
2 tablespoons chopped walnuts

4 to 6 servings

1 In a 2-quart casserole, combine the broccoli, onion, water and garlic. Cover. Microwave at High for 6 to 8 minutes, or until vegetables are tender-crisp, stirring once during cooking time.

2 Stir in the cooked macaroni, chicken, Italian seasoning and pepper. Re-cover. Microwave at High for 3 to 6 minutes, or until the mixture is heated through, stirring once during cooking time. Blend in the sour cream and Parmesan cheese. Sprinkle with walnuts before serving.

Total Cooking Time: 9 to 14 minutes

Italian Chicken Sauce

1 can (16 oz.) whole tomatoes
1 can (6 oz.) tomato paste
¼ cup water
1 small onion, finely chopped
1 medium carrot, shredded
2 cups cubed cooked chicken
½ teaspoon Italian seasoning
½ teaspoon sugar
¼ teaspoon salt
⅛ teaspoon pepper

4 servings

1 Combine all ingredients in a 1½-quart casserole, stirring to break apart tomatoes. Microwave at High for 3 minutes. Cover.

2 Microwave at 50% (Medium) for 10 to 15 minutes, or until the flavors are blended and sauce is hot and bubbly, stirring 2 or 3 times during cooking. Let stand for 5 minutes. If desired, serve over hot cooked noodles.

Total Cooking Time: 13 to 18 minutes

Wild Rice Casserole

    1 pkg. (6 oz.) long grain and wild rice mix
2⅓ cups hot tap water
    1 tablespoon butter
    1 pkg. (10 oz.) frozen chopped spinach
    2 cups cubed cooked chicken
  ½ cup sour cream

4 to 6 servings

1 In a 2-quart casserole, combine the rice and flavoring packet, hot water and butter. Cover. Microwave at High for 5 minutes. Microwave at 50% (Medium) for 15 to 25 minutes longer, or until the liquid is absorbed and rice is tender. Let stand, covered, for 10 minutes.

2 Unwrap spinach and place on a plate. Microwave spinach at High for 4 to 6 minutes, or until defrosted, turning over and breaking apart once during cooking time. Drain thoroughly, pressing to remove excess moisture. Stir the spinach and cubed chicken into rice; re-cover.

3 Microwave at High for 4 to 5 minutes, or until the mixture is hot. Stir in the sour cream. Let the casserole stand, covered, for 3 minutes before serving.

Total Cooking Time: 28 to 40 minutes

Chicken à la King ▲

  ¼ cup butter or margarine
    3 tablespoons all-purpose flour
    1 can (10¾ oz.) condensed chicken broth
      Milk
    2 cups cubed cooked chicken
  ¼ teaspoon pepper
    1 cup frozen peas
    1 can (4 oz.) sliced mushrooms, drained
      Toast points

4 to 6 servings

1 In a 2-quart casserole, microwave the butter at High for 1¼ to 1½ minutes, or until melted. Stir in the flour. Set aside.

2 In a 2-cup measure, combine chicken broth with enough milk to equal 1¾ cups. Blend the broth and milk mixture into the flour mixture. Microwave at High for 5½ to 7½ minutes, or until mixture thickens and bubbles, stirring once or twice during cooking time.

3 Stir in the remaining ingredients, except the toast points. Microwave at High for 2 to 4 minutes, or until mixture is hot, stirring once during cooking time. Serve over toast points.

Total Cooking Time: 8¾ to 13 minutes

Chicken Enchiladas

Filling:
- 2 cups cubed cooked chicken
- 1 cup ricotta or cottage cheese
- ½ teaspoon salt
- ⅛ teaspoon pepper
- ½ cup chopped ripe olives
- 8 corn tortillas (6-inch diameter) softened according to pkg. directions

Sauce:
- 1¼ cups prepared mild salsa sauce
- 2 tablespoons tomato paste
- 2 tablespoons chopped green pepper (optional)

Topping:
- 1½ cups shredded Cheddar cheese

4 servings

Follow photo directions, right.

Total Cooking Time: 10 to 16 minutes

How to Microwave Chicken Enchiladas

1 Combine filling ingredients in a medium bowl; mix well. Divide filling into 8 equal portions, then place 1 portion down the center of each corn tortilla.

2 Roll up each tortilla to enclose filling. Arrange enchiladas seam-side-down in 9-inch square baking dish. Blend sauce ingredients in a small bowl; pour over enchiladas.

3 Cover the baking dish with wax paper. Microwave at High for 7 to 11 minutes, or until the enchiladas are heated through, rotating the dish once during cooking time.

4 Sprinkle enchiladas with cheese. Microwave at 50% (Medium) for 3 to 5 minutes, or until cheese melts, rotating dish once during cooking time. Let stand for 3 minutes before serving.

Sweet & Sour Chicken

1 pkg. (6 oz.) frozen pea pods
2 tablespoons water
1 can (20 oz.) pineapple chunks, drained
   (reserve juice)
2 cups cubed cooked chicken
1 cup thinly sliced celery
1 small onion, thinly sliced
¼ cup chopped green pepper
4 teaspoons cornstarch
1 tablespoon packed brown sugar
1 teaspoon instant chicken bouillon granules
¼ teaspoon salt
   Dash ground ginger
1½ tablespoons soy sauce
1 tablespoon vinegar

4 servings

1 Place the pea pods and water in a 2-quart casserole. Cover. Microwave at High for 2 to 4 minutes, or until the pea pods are defrosted, stirring to break apart once during cooking time. Drain. Stir in the pineapple chunks, chicken, celery, onion and green pepper. Set aside.

2 In a 4-cup measure, combine the cornstarch, bouillon, ginger, salt and brown sugar. Stir in the soy sauce, vinegar and reserved pineapple juice. Microwave at High for 2 to 5 minutes, or until the sauce is clear and thickened, stirring 2 or 3 times during cooking.

3 Pour the sauce over the chicken mixture; stir to combine. Cover. Microwave at High for 4 to 8 minutes, or until the vegetables are tender-crisp, stirring twice during cooking time.

Total Cooking Time: 8 to 17 minutes

Serving Tip:
Serve Sweet & Sour Chicken over hot cooked rice or crunchy chow mein noodles.

Chicken Chow Mein ➤

2 tablespoons cornstarch
¼ cup water
1 can (16 oz.) chow mein vegetables
1 pkg. (8 oz.) mushrooms, sliced
2 cups cubed cooked chicken
1 cup thinly sliced celery
1 small onion, chopped
2 tablespoons soy sauce
2 teaspoons instant chicken bouillon granules
½ cup chow mein noodles

4 servings

1 Blend the cornstarch and water in a 2-quart casserole. Add remaining ingredients, except the chow mein noodles. Cover.

2 Microwave at High for 12 to 17 minutes, or until the sauce is clear and thickened and the vegetables are tender-crisp, stirring 3 times during cooking. Top with chow mein noodles. If desired, serve with hot cooked rice.

Total Cooking Time: 12 to 17 minutes

Oriental Chicken

2 cups cubed cooked chicken
2 cups uncooked instant rice
1 pkg. (10 oz.) frozen stir-fry vegetables
    with seasoning
1 cup water
3 tablespoons soy sauce
1 teaspoon instant chicken bouillon granules

4 servings

Combine all ingredients in a 2-quart casserole. Cover. Microwave at High for 12 to 14 minutes, or until the rice is tender and liquid is absorbed, stirring once during cooking time. Let stand for 3 minutes; stir before serving.

Total Cooking Time: 12 to 14 minutes

Make Ahead Meals

*Spend a few minutes today,
and save hours in days to come*

Basic Chicken Mix

2 whole broiler-fryer chickens (2½ to 3 lbs.
   each) cut into 8 pieces each, skin removed
3 tablespoons all-purpose flour
1 medium onion, chopped
1 small carrot, finely chopped
1 tablespoon instant chicken bouillon granules
1 tablespoon dried parsley flakes
¾ teaspoon salt
½ teaspoon dried basil leaves
½ teaspoon dried marjoram leaves

                                2 containers mix

Follow photo directions, right.

Total Cooking Time: 29 to 36 minutes

How to Microwave Basic Chicken Mix

1 Arrange the chicken pieces in layers in a
3-quart casserole, sprinkling each layer with
flour. Sprinkle the remaining ingredients over the
chicken. Cover.

2 Microwave at High for 29 to 36 minutes, or
until meat near bone is no longer pink and
juices run clear, rearranging pieces 3 or 4 times
during cooking. Remove chicken from the bones;
discard bones.

3 Dice meat and set aside. Skim the fat from
broth; return chicken meat to the broth.
Divide mixture into 2 portions; use 1 portion
immediately in a recipe, or freeze both for future
use (right).

Quick Chicken Pilaf

½ cup chopped celery
½ cup chopped green pepper
2 teaspoons olive or vegetable oil
1 container Basic Chicken Mix, defrosted (below)
1½ cups uncooked instant rice
1 cup chicken broth
¼ teaspoon salt
⅓ cup raisins (optional)
½ cup cashews or peanuts

4 to 6 servings

1 Combine the celery, green pepper and oil in a 2-quart casserole. Cover. Microwave at High for 2 to 3 minutes, or until vegetables are tender-crisp.

2 Stir in the Basic Chicken Mix, rice, broth and salt. Re-cover. Microwave at High for 7 to 10 minutes, or until the rice is tender and liquid is absorbed, stirring once during cooking time. Stir in the raisins; sprinkle with cashews. Let stand, covered, for 2 to 3 minutes before serving.

Total Cooking Time: 9 to 13 minutes

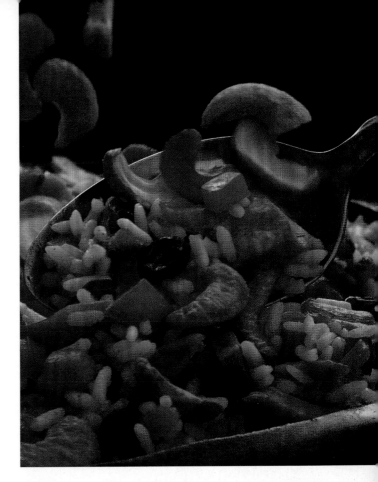

How to Freeze and Defrost Basic Chicken Mix

Spoon chicken-and-sauce mixture into 2 equal portions. Place in freezer containers, label and freeze for future use in recipes.

Defrost 1 container chicken mix in a 1-quart casserole. Microwave at 50% (Medium) for 8 to 14 minutes, or until mix is still cold but no longer icy, stirring occasionally. Let stand for 5 minutes.

Chicken & Broccoli with Spaghetti

  1 pkg. (10 oz.) frozen chopped broccoli
  ¼ cup butter or margarine
  ¼ cup all-purpose flour
  ½ teaspoon salt
  ¼ teaspoon onion powder
  ⅛ teaspoon pepper
    Dash garlic powder
2¼ cups milk
  1 container frozen Basic Chicken Mix,
     defrosted (page 79)
  ¼ cup grated Parmesan cheese
  1 pkg. (7 oz.) uncooked spaghetti, prepared
     as directed on pkg.

4 to 6 servings

1 Unwrap the broccoli and place on a plate. Microwave at High for 4 to 6 minutes, or until broccoli is defrosted, turning over and breaking apart once during cooking time. Drain; set aside.

2 In a 2-quart casserole, microwave butter at High for 1¼ to 1½ minutes, or until melted. Stir in the flour, salt, onion powder, pepper, and garlic powder. Blend in the milk.

3 Microwave at High for 6 to 11 minutes, or until the mixture thickens and boils, stirring 4 or 5 times during cooking.

4 Add the broccoli and Basic Chicken Mix. Microwave at High for 2 to 4 minutes, or until the sauce is heated through, stirring once during cooking time.

5 Serve the sauce over hot cooked spaghetti; sprinkle with Parmesan cheese.

Total Cooking Time: 13¼ to 22½ minutes

Chicken Paprikash

1½ cups sliced fresh mushrooms
½ cup thinly sliced celery
1 small onion, sliced
1 tablespoon butter or margarine
⅛ teaspoon instant minced garlic
1 container frozen Basic Chicken Mix,
   defrosted (page 79)
1½ teaspoons paprika
½ teaspoon salt
½ cup sour cream

4 servings

1 In a 1½-quart casserole, combine the mushrooms, celery, onion, butter and garlic. Cover. Microwave at High for 4 to 7 minutes, or until the celery is tender, stirring once during cooking time. Drain.

2 Mix in the remaining ingredients, except the sour cream. Cover. Microwave at High for 3 to 5 minutes, or until mixture is thoroughly heated, stirring once during cooking time.

3 Blend in the sour cream. Microwave at 50% (Medium) for 30 seconds to 1½ minutes, or until mixture is heated through.

Total Cooking Time: 7½ to 13½ minutes

Chicken Stew with Dumplings

Stew:

- 1 container frozen Basic Chicken Mix, defrosted (page 79)
- 3 tablespoons all-purpose flour
- 2 cups cubed potatoes (½-inch cubes)
- 1 can (10¾ oz.) condensed chicken broth
- 1 cup thinly sliced carrot
- ¼ cup water
- ⅛ teaspoon pepper
- ⅛ teaspoon dried rosemary leaves (optional)
- 1 cup frozen peas

Dumplings:

- 1½ cups buttermilk baking mix
- 2 teaspoons poppy seed (optional)
- 1 teaspoon dried parsley flakes
- ½ cup milk
- 1 teaspoon wheat germ (optional)

4 servings

Follow photo directions, right.

Total Cooking Time: 24 to 37 minutes

How to Microwave Chicken Stew with Dumplings

1 Place defrosted Basic Chicken Mix in 3-quart casserole. Add flour and remaining stew ingredients, except peas; stir to combine. Cover.

2 Microwave at High for 20 to 30 minutes, or until vegetables are tender, stirring once. Stir in the frozen peas. Cover and set aside.

3 Combine dumpling ingredients, except wheat germ, in a medium bowl. Drop 8 tablespoons of the dumpling mix in a ring on top of the stew. Sprinkle dumplings with wheat germ.

4 Microwave at High for 4 to 7 minutes, or until the dumplings are light and springy to the touch, rotating dish 2 or 3 times during cooking.

◄ Chicken Macaroni Bake

1½ cups frozen cut green beans
1½ cups frozen cauliflowerets
 2 tablespoons water
 1 container frozen Basic Chicken Mix,
    defrosted (page 79)
 ¾ cup uncooked elbow macaroni, prepared as
    directed on pkg.
 1 cup shredded Cheddar cheese, divided
 1 can (10¾ oz.) condensed cream of
    mushroom soup
 1 teaspoon lemon juice
 ½ teaspoon dry mustard
 1 tablespoon dry bread crumbs

4 to 6 servings

1 Combine the green beans, cauliflowerets and water in a 2-quart casserole. Cover. Microwave at High for 6 to 9 minutes, or until the vegetables are tender, stirring once during cooking time. Cut large cauliflowerets into smaller pieces.

2 Stir in Basic Chicken Mix, macaroni, ¾ cup of the cheese, mushroom soup, lemon juice and mustard. Microwave at High for 7 minutes. Stir.

3 Sprinkle the bread crumbs and the remaining cheese over the chicken mixture. Microwave at High for 2 to 3½ minutes, or until mixture is heated through and cheese is melted.

Total Cooking Time: 15 to 19½ minutes

Stewed Chicken Mix

2½ to 3-lb. whole broiler-fryer chicken, cut into
    8 pieces, skin removed
 2 cups hot tap water
 1 stalk celery, chopped
 1 small onion, chopped
 1 small carrot, chopped
 1 teaspoon salt
 ¼ teaspoon pepper
 ¼ teaspoon garlic powder

2 containers

1 Combine chicken and remaining ingredients in a 3-quart casserole; cover. Microwave at High for 25 to 32 minutes, or until meat near the bone is no longer pink and the juices run clear, rearranging chicken 2 or 3 times during cooking.

2 Remove chicken from broth. Remove chicken meat from bones; dice meat and set aside. Discard bones; return chicken meat to broth in casserole. Divide chicken and broth into 2 equal portions. Use one portion immediately in one of the following recipes; or spoon both portions into freezer containers, label and freeze.

3 To defrost: In a 2-quart casserole, microwave 1 container of the frozen stewed chicken at 50% (Medium) for 6 to 12 minutes, or until mixture is still cold but no longer icy, stirring to break apart several times during cooking. Let mix stand for 5 minutes to complete defrosting.

Total Cooking Time: 25 to 32 minutes

Creamy Chicken & Artichokes ➤

1 pkg. (9 oz.) frozen artichoke hearts
1 container Stewed Chicken Mix, defrosted
   (opposite)
¼ cup all-purpose flour
¾ cup milk
2 tablespoons chopped pimiento
½ teaspoon salt
¼ teaspoon paprika
1 tablespoon butter or margarine
¼ cup sliced almonds
4 frozen patty shells, prepared as directed
   on pkg.

4 servings

1 Unwrap artichoke hearts and place on a plate. Microwave at High for 3 to 4 minutes, or until the artichokes are defrosted, turning over and breaking apart once during cooking time. Drain; set aside.

2 Place the defrosted Stewed Chicken Mix in a 2-quart casserole. In a small bowl, blend the flour with a small amount of broth from the stew mix. Add flour mixture back to the stew mix; blend in the milk. Stir in artichoke hearts, pimiento, salt and paprika.

3 Microwave at High for 11 to 18 minutes, or until mixture thickens and bubbles, stirring 4 or 5 times during cooking. Cover casserole to keep warm. Set aside.

4 In a medium bowl, microwave the butter and almonds at High for 3½ to 5 minutes, or until almonds are lightly browned, stirring once or twice during cooking time. Drain almonds on paper towels, then add to the chicken mixture. To serve, spoon chicken-artichoke mixture into patty shells.

Total Cooking Time: 17½ to 27 minutes

Serving Variation:
Instead of serving Creamy Chicken & Artichokes in patty shells, toss with hot cooked fettuccine. Sprinkle with grated Parmesan cheese before serving.

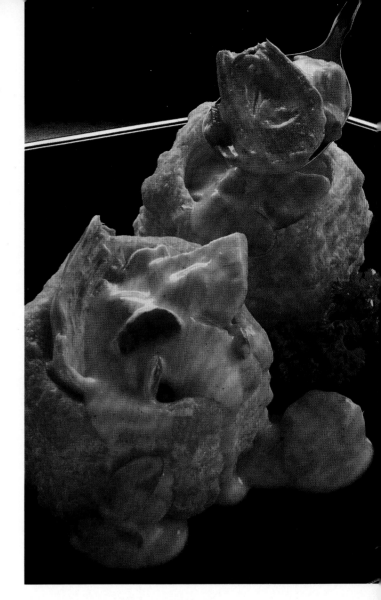

Hearty Chicken Soup

1 container Stewed Chicken Mix, defrosted
   (opposite)
1 pkg. (10 oz.) frozen chopped broccoli,
   or mixed vegetables
1¾ cups chicken broth
1 cup uncooked instant rice
¼ teaspoon salt
⅛ teaspoon pepper

4 to 6 servings

Combine all ingredients in a 2-quart casserole. Cover; microwave at High for 13 to 17 minutes, or until rice and vegetables are tender, stirring once during cooking time. Let casserole stand for 3 minutes before serving.

Total Cooking Time: 13 to 17 minutes

Chicken with Sour Cream Sauce

2½ to 3-lb. whole broiler-fryer chicken, cut
    into 8 pieces, skin removed
 2 medium carrots, thinly sliced
 ½ cup thinly sliced celery
 ¼ cup chopped onion
 ½ teaspoon salt
 ¼ teaspoon pepper
 ¼ teaspoon dried thyme leaves
 1 can (10¾ oz.) condensed cream of
    chicken soup
 ½ cup water

At serving time:
 ½ cup sour cream

4 to 6 servings

1 In a 3-quart casserole, combine the chicken, carrots, celery, onion, salt, pepper and thyme. Mix the soup and water in a small bowl; pour mixture over chicken and vegetables. Cover.

2 Microwave at High for 22 to 30 minutes, or until meat near the bone is no longer pink and the juices run clear, rearranging and turning chicken over 2 or 3 times during cooking.

3 Spoon the mixture into a freezer container, label and freeze for future use.

Total Cooking Time: 22 to 30 minutes

To serve:
Place frozen portion in a 2-quart casserole. Cover; microwave at High for 5 minutes. Stir to break apart. Microwave at 50% (Medium) for 20 to 25 minutes longer, or until heated, stirring to break apart and rearranging pieces twice during cooking time. Remove chicken pieces from sauce; set aside. Blend the sour cream into sauce; spoon the sauce mixture over chicken. If desired, serve with hot cooked noodles.

Paella

1 cup chopped green pepper
1 cup chopped onion
2 tablespoons olive or vegetable oil
⅛ teaspoon instant minced garlic
1 can (16 oz.) whole tomatoes, cut up
1 can (10¾ oz.) condensed chicken broth
1 cup cubed fully cooked ham (½-inch cubes)
½ teaspoon paprika
1 small bay leaf (optional)
⅛ teaspoon ground saffron or turmeric
⅛ teaspoon cayenne
2½ to 3-lb. whole broiler-fryer chicken, cut into
    8 pieces
½ lb. medium shrimp (uncooked) peeled and
    deveined
1 can (8 oz.) whole oysters, drained
    (optional)

To serve 1 portion:

2 cups hot cooked rice
1 cup frozen peas

2 containers

1 In a 3-quart casserole, combine the green pepper, onion, oil and garlic. Cover; microwave at High for 5 to 8 minutes, or until vegetables are tender-crisp, stirring once during cooking time.

2 Stir in the tomatoes, broth, ham, paprika, bay leaf, saffron and cayenne. Add the chicken; re-cover. Microwave at High for 22 to 28 minutes, or until meat near bone is no longer pink and the juices run clear, stirring to rearrange chicken twice during cooking time.

3 Skim fat from casserole. Stir in the shrimp and oysters. Divide mixture into 2 portions; spoon into 2 freezer containers, label and freeze.

Total Cooking Time: 27 to 36 minutes

To serve:
Place one portion of frozen Paella in a 3-quart casserole. Cover; microwave at High for 10 to 15 minutes, or until chicken pieces can be separated. Stir in the rice and peas; re-cover. Microwave at 50% (Medium) for 15 to 23 minutes, or until shrimp is firm and opaque and mixture is heated, stirring once or twice during cooking time. Let stand for 5 minutes.

Stuffed Chicken Breast a L'Orange

2 whole boneless chicken breasts (1¼ to 1½ lbs.) cut into 4 breast halves, skin removed

Stuffing:

¼ cup finely chopped celery
3 tablespoons butter or margarine
2 tablespoons sliced green onion
2 tablespoons raisins
2 tablespoons orange juice
½ cup unseasoned dry bread crumbs
½ teaspoon grated orange peel
⅛ teaspoon garlic powder

Sauce:

½ cup orange juice
1½ teaspoons cornstarch
2 tablespoons raisins
1½ teaspoons packed brown sugar
⅛ teaspoon ground cinnamon
4 thin orange slices

2 to 4 servings

Follow photo directions, below.

Total Cooking Time: 19½ to 30½ minutes

How to Microwave Stuffed Chicken Breast a L'Orange

1 Pound breast halves to ¼-inch thickness; set aside. Combine celery, butter and green onion in 1-quart casserole. Cover; microwave at High for 1½ to 3 minutes, or until vegetables are tender-crisp, stirring once or twice during cooking time. Stir in raisins and 2 tablespoons orange juice.

2 Stir the remaining stuffing ingredients into the casserole; mix well. Place about ¼ cup of the stuffing mixture at ends of breast halves. Roll up each breast to enclose stuffing; secure with wooden picks. Wrap stuffed breasts individually, label and freeze for future use.

3 *To serve*, unwrap frozen chicken breasts. Place in a 9-inch square baking dish. Cover with wax paper. Microwave at 50% (Medium) for 16 to 24 minutes, or until chicken is no longer pink in center, rotating the dish 3 or 4 times during cooking. Set aside.

4 Mix ½ cup orange juice and cornstarch in a medium bowl. Stir in the remaining sauce ingredients, except orange slices. Microwave at High for 2 to 3½ minutes, or until sauce is clear and thickened, stirring once or twice during cooking time. To serve, spoon sauce over chicken breasts; top with orange slices.

No Time to Cook?

Eating can still be fun

Convenience chicken products are fully cooked and need to be microwaved only until heated. Some have been seasoned or breaded for you. Be sure to choose chicken patties, nuggets and cutlets with a toasted bread crumb coating; these convenience products can be microwaved without prior defrosting.

Frozen Convenience Chicken Products

Product:	Amount:	Time at High:	Directions:
Fried Chicken	2-3 pieces	2½-5 minutes	Arrange chicken pieces on roasting rack with meaty portions toward outside. Cover with a paper towel. Rearrange once during cooking time. Microwave until hot (145°F).
	4 pieces	4-9 minutes	
	9-11 pieces	15-20 minutes	
Breaded Chicken Patties	2 patties	4-4½ minutes	Place chicken patties on roasting rack. Microwave at High for 2 minutes. Turn patties over and microwave for remaining time or until hot, rotating once during cooking time.
	4 patties	5-6½ minutes	
Breaded Chicken Chunks	16-22 pieces	6-8 minutes	Arrange chicken pieces on roasting rack. Microwave at High until hot, rearranging pieces once during cooking time.
Chicken Kiev or Cordon Bleu (pictured above)	1 serving (6 oz.)	4-6 minutes	Remove plastic overwrap. Place on roasting rack or trivet. Rotate dish once during cooking time. Microwave until hot (145°F).
	2 servings (6 oz. each)	5-8 minutes	

Saucy Fried Chicken ➤

1 cup prepared barbecue sauce
1 cup orange marmalade or pineapple
  preserves
1 envelope (1¼ oz.) onion soup mix
1 pkg. (32 oz.) frozen fried chicken

4 to 6 servings

1 Combine the barbecue sauce, marmalade and
soup mix in a medium bowl. Microwave at
High for 3 to 5 minutes, or until the onion is
tender and mixture is heated, stirring once
during cooking time.

2 Arrange frozen chicken on a roasting rack.
Brush with the sauce. Microwave at High for
15 to 20 minutes, or until hot (145°F), rearranging
and brushing pieces with sauce once during
cooking time.

Total Cooking Time: 18 to 25 minutes

Variation:

Saucy Deli Chicken:
Follow recipe for Saucy Fried Chicken except:
substitute 9 to 11 pieces of deli fried chicken
for frozen chicken. Microwave at High for 2 to
5 minutes, or until hot (145°F), rearranging
and brushing pieces with sauce once during
cooking time.

◄ Chicken Romanoff

1 pkg. (10 oz.) frozen chopped spinach
1 pkg. (5½ oz.) noodles Romanoff mix,
   prepared as directed on pkg.
2 cans (5 oz. each) chunked chicken
1 cup shredded Swiss cheese
¼ teaspoon poultry seasoning
2 tablespoons grated Parmesan cheese
¼ cup sliced almonds

4 servings

1 Unwrap spinach and place on a plate; micro-wave at High for 4 to 6 minutes, or until defrosted, turning over and breaking apart once during cooking time. Drain, pressing to remove excess moisture; set aside. In a medium bowl, combine noodles Romanoff, spinach, chicken, Swiss cheese and poultry seasoning.

2 Spoon mixture into a 1½-quart casserole. Sprinkle with Parmesan cheese. Microwave at 50% (Medium) for 12 to 19 minutes, or until mixture is heated, rotating dish once or twice during cooking time. Sprinkle with almonds.

Total Cooking Time: 16 to 25 minutes

Cheesy Chicken Patties

2 frozen breaded chicken patties
2 slices (¾ oz. each) American cheese
2 toasted hamburger buns
Additional Toppings:
   Sliced tomato
   Sliced onion
   Sliced avocado
   Lettuce
   Mayonnaise

2 servings

1 Arrange frozen chicken patties on a roasting rack. Microwave at High for 2 minutes. Turn patties over. Microwave at High for 2 to 2½ minutes longer, or until patties are hot.

2 Top patties with cheese slices. Microwave at High for 45 seconds to 1¼ minutes, or until cheese melts. Serve patties on toasted buns with desired toppings.

Total Cooking Time: 4¾ to 5¾ minutes

Sweet & Sour Chicken Chunks ►

½ cup cubed green pepper (¾-inch cubes)
1 small onion, chopped
1 small carrot, thinly sliced
2 tablespoons butter or margarine
⅛ teaspoon pepper
½ cup prepared sweet & sour sauce
¼ cup apricot preserves
1 tablespoon soy sauce
1 pkg. (12 oz.) frozen breaded chicken chunks

4 servings

1 In a 1½-quart casserole, combine the green pepper, onion, carrot, butter and pepper. Cover. Microwave at High for 4 to 6 minutes, or until the vegetables are tender-crisp, stirring twice during cooking time.

2 Add the sweet & sour sauce, preserves and soy sauce. Add the chicken chunks, stirring to coat with sauce. Microwave at High for 6 to 10 minutes, or until chicken is hot and sauce is bubbly, stirring 2 or 3 times during cooking. If desired, serve over hot cooked rice.

Total Cooking Time: 10 to 16 minutes

Quick Chicken & Rice

1 tablespoon butter or margarine
1 can (10¾ oz.) condensed cream of
   mushroom soup
1 can (10¾ oz.) condensed cream of
   celery soup
½ cup milk
2 cups uncooked instant rice
8 pieces take-out or deli fried chicken

4 servings

1 In a 10-inch square baking dish, microwave the butter at High for 45 seconds to 1 minute, or until melted. Add the soups and milk; stir in rice. Cover dish with plastic wrap. Microwave at High for 6 to 9 minutes, or until rice is tender.

2 Arrange chicken over rice mixture, with meaty portions toward outside edges of dish. Microwave at High for 5 to 8 minutes, or until chicken is heated, stirring and rearranging pieces once during cooking time. (If chicken was refrigerated, increase microwave time to 8 to 13 minutes.)

Total Cooking Time: 11¾ to 18 minutes

INDEX

CY DE COSSE INCORPORATED
Chairman: Cy DeCosse
President: James B. Maus
Executive Vice President: William B. Jones

CREDITS
Design, Production & Photography:
  Cy DeCosse Incorporated
Art Directors: Bill Nelson, Bill Jones
Project Managers: Lynette Reber, Sue Kersten
Home Economists: Peggy Lamb, Jill Crum,
  Kathy Weber
Production Manager: Jim Bindas
Assistant Production Manager: Julie Churchill
Copy Editor: Bryan Trandem
Typesetting: Jennie Smith, Linda Schloegel
Production Staff: Yelena Konrardy, Lisa
  Rosenthal, David Schelitzche, Cathleen
  Shannon, Nik Wogstad, Michelle Joy
Photographers: Tony Kubat, John
  Lauenstein, Mette Nielsen
Food Stylists: Teresa Rys, Susan Sinon,
  Suzanne Finley, Robin Krause,
  Susan Zechmann
Production Consultant: Christine Watkins
Special Microwave Consultant:
  Barbara Methven
Color Separations: La Cromolito
Printing: R.R. Donnelley & Sons (1186)

A

Arroz Con Pollo, 39
Artichokes,
  Creamy Chicken & Artichokes, 85

B

Barbecue,
  Barbecued Chicken Drumsticks, 15
  Outdoor Barbecued Chicken
    Pieces, 15
Basic Chicken Mix, 78
Beans,
  Marinated Chicken & Bean Salad, 63
Boning,
  How to Bone a Half Chicken
    Breast, 28
Bran-Herb Coated Chicken, 20
Breaded Chicken Chunks,
  Frozen, 90
Breaded Chicken Patties,
  Frozen, 90
Breasts, 26-41
  Arroz con Polo, 39
  Chicken & Broccoli, 36
  Chicken & Pea Pods, 36
  Chicken Breasts in Mushroom
    Sauce, 33
  Chicken Imperial, 40
  Cinnamon-Orange Spiced Chicken, 31
  Citrus Marinated Chicken, 29
  Crab-stuffed Chicken Breasts, 41
  Cranberry-Orange Glazed Chicken, 31
  Lemon-seasoned Chicken Breasts 29
  Mexican Chicken, 32
  Oriental Chicken with Peanut
    Sauce, 38
  Raspberry-Lemon Sauced Chicken, 30
  Sunday Chicken Bake, 34
  Tarragon Chicken, 41
Broccoli,
  Chicken & Broccoli, 36
  Chicken & Broccoli with Spaghetti, 80

C

Canned Chicken, 6
Cashews,
  Cashew-coated Chicken, 20
  Shredded Chicken & Cashews, 71
Casseroles,
  Chicken & Rice Casserole, 24
  Chicken Macaroni Bake, 84
  Chicken Romanoff, 92
  Paella, 87
  Quick Chicken Pilaf, 79
  Walnut Pasta & Chicken, 72
  Wild Rice Casserole, 73
Cheddar Cheese,
  Chicken-Cheddar Soup, 61

Cheesy Chicken Patties, 92
Chicken,
  see: Breasts, Casseroles, Creative
    Leftovers, Make Ahead Meals,
    Pieces, Salads, Soups & Stews,
    Whole Chicken
  Basic Chicken Mix, 78
  Canned Chicken, 6
  Convenient Substitutes for Chicken, 7
  Deli Chicken, 6
  Fried Chicken,
    Frozen, 90
  Frozen Convenience Chicken
    Products, 90
  How to Bone a Half Chicken
    Breast, 28
  How to Microwave a Whole
    Chicken, 44
  How to Microwave Chicken Pieces, 12
  How to Microwave Coated Chicken
    Pieces, 18
  How to Prepare Chicken for
    Microwaving, 8
  How to Select Chicken, 5
  How to Test Microwave Chicken for
    Doneness, 8
  Chicken à la King, 73
  Chicken & Broccoli, 36
  Chicken & Broccoli with Spaghetti, 80
  Chicken & Pea Pods, 36
  Chicken & Rice Casserole, 24
  Chicken & Spinach Salad, 67
  Chicken Basics, 8-9
  Chicken Breasts in Mushroom
    Sauce, 33
  Chicken-Cheddar Soup, 61
  Chicken Chili, 55
  Chicken Chow Mein, 77
  Chicken Enchiladas, 74
  Chicken Imperial, 40
  Chicken in Lemon-Wine Sauce, 22
  Chicken Kiev,
    Frozen, 90
  Chicken Macaroni Bake, 84
  Chicken-Okra Gumbo, 56
  Chicken Paprikash, 81
  Chicken Romanoff, 92
  Chicken Stew, 53
  Chicken Stew with Dumplings, 82
  Chicken-stuffed Tomatoes, 71
  Chicken with Sour Cream Sauce, 86
Chili,
  Chicken Chili, 55
Chow Mein,
  Chicken Chow Mein, 77
Cinnamon-Orange Spiced Chicken, 31
Citrus Marinated Chicken, 29
Classic Herb Chicken, 23
Coatings, 18-25
  see: Quick Coatings for Chicken
    Pieces

94

Convenience Foods,
  Frozen Convenience Chicken
    Products, 90
  Super Convenience, 6-7
Convenient Substitutes for Cooked
  Chicken, 7
Coq Au Vin, 25
Cordon Bleu,
  Frozen, 90
Crab-stuffed Chicken Breasts, 41
Crackers,
  Savory Cracker-coated Chicken, 18
Cranberry-Orange Glazed Chicken, 31
Creamy Chicken & Artichokes, 85
Creative Leftovers, 70-77
  Chicken à la King, 73
  Chicken Chow Mein, 77
  Chicken Enchiladas, 74
  Chicken-stuffed Tomatoes, 71
  Italian Chicken Sauce, 72
  Oriental Chicken, 77
  Shredded Chicken & Cashews, 71
  Sweet & Sour Chicken, 76
  Walnut Pasta & Chicken, 72
  Wild Rice Casserole, 73
Crunchy Chicken Salad, 66

D

Deli Chicken, 6
Doneness,
  How to Test Microwave Chicken for
    Doneness, 9
Drumsticks,
  Barbecued Chicken Drumsticks, 15
Dumplings,
  Chicken Stew with Dumplings, 82

E

Enchiladas,
  Chicken Enchiladas, 74

F

Freezing,
  How to Freeze Poultry, 8-9
Fried Chicken,
  Frozen, 90
  Saucy Fried Chicken, with
    Variation, 91
Fried Onion Ring Coating, 18
Frozen Convenience Chicken
  Products, 90
Frozen Poultry, 7

G

Garlic,
  Soy-Garlic Glazed Chicken, 48
Ginger,
  Sesame-Ginger Chicken, 21

Glaze,
  Cranberry-Orange Glazed Chicken, 31
  Orange Glazed Chicken, 16
  Pineapple Glazed Chicken, 48
  Soy-Garlic Glazed Chicken, 48
Gumbo,
  Chicken-Okra Gumbo, 56-57

H

Hearty Chicken Soup, 85
Herb,
  Bran-Herb Coated Chicken, 20
  Classic Herb Chicken, 23
  Herb-roasted Chicken, 47
Herbed Coating, 18
Hot Chicken Salad, 66
Hot Chicken Waldorf Sandwiches, 69
Hot Chicken Waldorf, with
  Variation, 69

I

Italian Chicken Sauce, 72
Italian Style Sauce, 15

L

Leftovers,
  see: Creative Leftovers, 70-77
Lemon,
  Chicken in Lemon-Wine Sauce, 22
  Lemon-seasoned Chicken Breasts, 29
  Raspberry-Lemon Sauced Chicken, 30
Lemony Chicken Soup, 60
Light Crumb Coating, 18

M

Macaroni,
  Chicken Macaroni Bake, 84
Make Ahead Meals, 78-89
  Basic Chicken Mix, 78
  Chicken & Broccoli with Spaghetti, 80
  Chicken Macaroni Bake, 84
  Chicken Paprikash, 81
  Chicken Stew with Dumplings, 82
  Chicken with Sour Cream Sauce, 86
  Creamy Chicken & Artichokes, 85
  Hearty Chicken Soup, 85
  Paella, 87
  Quick Chicken Pilaf, 79
  Stewed Chicken Mix, 84
  Stuffed Chicken Breast a L'Orange, 88
Marinated Chicken & Bean Salad, 63
Mediterranean Chicken Salad, 65
Melon,
  Tropical Chicken-Melon Salad, 64
Mexican Chicken, 32

Mexican Style Sauce, 15
Mixes,
  Basic Chicken Mix, 78
  Stewed Chicken Mix, 84
Mushrooms,
  Chicken Breasts in Mushroom
    Sauce, 33

N

No Time to Cook, 90-93
  Cheesy Chicken Patties, 92
  Chicken Romanoff, 92
  Frozen Convenience Chicken
    Products, 90
  Quick Chicken & Rice, 93
  Saucy Fried Chicken, with
    Variation, 91
  Sweet & Sour Chicken Chunks, 93
Noodles,
  Old-fashioned Chicken-Noodle
    Soup, 54
  Roast Chicken with Noodles, 49

O

Okra,
  Chicken-Okra Gumbo, 56
Old-fashioned Chicken-Noodle
  Soup, 54
Onions,
  Fried Onion Ring Coating, 18
Orange,
  Cinnamon-Orange Spiced Chicken, 31
  Cranberry-Orange Glazed Chicken, 31
  Orange Blossom Sauce, 15
  Orange Glazed Chicken, 16
  Stuffed Chicken Breast a L'Orange, 88
Oriental Chicken, 77
Oriental Chicken with Peanut Sauce, 38
Outdoor Barbecued Chicken Pieces, 15

P

Paella, 87
Paprikash,
  Chicken Paprikash, 81
Pasta,
  Walnut Pasta & Chicken, 72
Patties,
  Breaded Chicken Patties,
    Frozen, 90
  Cheesy Chicken Patties, 92
Pea Pods,
  Chicken & Pea Pods, 36
Peanuts,
  Oriental Chicken with Peanut
    Sauce, 38
Pieces,
  Chicken & Rice Casserole, 24
  Chicken in Lemon-Wine Sauce, 22
  Chicken Pieces, 10-13

Classic Herb Chicken, 23
Coq Au Vin, 25
Outdoor Barbecued Chicken
  Pieces, 15
Quick Coatings for Chicken
  Pieces, 18-25
Simple Saucy Chicken, 14-17
Speedy Chicken Stew, 23
Pilaf,
  Quick Chicken Pilaf, 79
Pineapple Glazed Chicken, 48
Poultry, 4-5
  Frozen Poultry, 7
  How to Freeze Poultry, 8-9

Q

Quick & Easy Sauce Ideas, 15
Quick Chicken & Rice, 93
Quick Chicken & Wild Rice Soup, 58
Quick Chicken Pilaf, 79
**Quick Coatings for Chicken
  Pieces,** 18-25
  Bran-Herb Coated Chicken, 20
  Cashew-coated Chicken, 20
  Fried Onion Ring Coating, 18
  Herbed Coating, 18
  How to Microwave Coated Chicken
    Pieces, 18
  Light Crumb Coating, 18
  Savory Cracker-coated Chicken, with
    Variations, 18
  Sesame-Ginger Chicken, 21

R

Raspberry-Lemon Sauced Chicken, 30
Rice,
  Arroz Con Pollo, 39
  Chicken & Rice Casserole, 24
  Paella, 87
  Quick Chicken & Rice, 93
  Quick Chicken & Wild Rice Soup, 58
  Quick Chicken Pilaf, 79
  Savory Chicken & Rice Soup, 59
  Wild Rice Casserole, 73
Roast Chicken with Noodles, 49
Russian Style Sauce, 15

S

Salads, 62-69
  Chicken & Spinach Salad, 67
  Crunchy Chicken Salad, 66
  Hot Chicken Salad, 66
  Hot Chicken Waldorf, with
    Variation, 69
  Marinated Chicken & Bean Salad, 63
  Mediterranean Chicken Salad, 65
  Tropical Chicken-Melon Salad, 64

Salsa Chicken, 17
Sandwiches,
  Cheesy Chicken Patties, 92
  Hot Chicken Waldorf Sandwiches, 69
Sauces,
  Italian Chicken Sauce, 72
  Italian Style Sauce, 15
  Mexican Style Sauce, 15
  Orange Blossom Sauce, 15
  Quick & Easy Sauce Ideas, 15
  Russian Style Sauce, 15
  Sweet & Sour Sauce, 15
Saucy Deli Chicken, 91
Saucy Fried Chicken, with Variation, 91
Savory Chicken & Rice Soup, 59
Savory Cracker-coated Chicken, with
  Variations, 18
Selection,
  How to Select Chicken, 5
Sesame-Ginger Chicken, 21
Shredded Chicken & Cashews, 71
Simple Saucy Chicken, 14-17
  Barbecued Chicken Drumsticks, 15
  Orange-glazed Chicken, 16
  Outdoor Barbecued Chicken
    Pieces, 15
  Quick & Easy Sauce Ideas, 15
  Salsa Chicken, 17
Soups & Stews, 52-61
  Chicken-Cheddar Soup, 61
  Chicken Chili, 55
  Chicken-Okra Gumbo, 56
  Chicken Stew, 53
  Chicken Stew with Dumplings, 82
  Hearty Chicken Soup, 85
  Lemony Chicken Soup, 60
  Old-fashioned Chicken-Noodle
    Soup, 54
  Quick Chicken & Wild Rice Soup, 58
  Savory Chicken & Rice Soup, 59
  Speedy Chicken Stew, 23
Sour Cream,
  Chicken with Sour Cream Sauce, 86
Soy-Garlic Glazed Chicken, 48
Spaghetti,
  Chicken & Broccoli with Spaghetti, 80
Speedy Chicken Stew, 23
Spinach,
  Chicken & Spinach Salad, 67
Stewed Chicken Mix, 84
Stews,
  see: Soups & Stews
Stuffed Chicken Breast a L'Orange, 88
Stuffed Chicken Italiano, 50
Substitutions,
  Convenient Substitutions for Cooked
    Chicken, 7
Sunday Chicken Bake, 34
Super Convenience, 6-7
Sweet & Sour Chicken, 76
Sweet & Sour Chicken Chunks, 93
Sweet & Sour Sauce, 15

T

Tarragon Chicken, 41
Tomatoes,
  Chicken-stuffed Tomatoes, 71
Tropical Chicken-Melon Salad, 64
Turkey,
  Fresh Turkey, 6

V

Vegetable-stuffed Chicken, 45

W

Walnut Pasta & Chicken, 72
Whole Chicken, 42-51
  Herb-roasted Chicken, 47
  How to Microwave a Whole
    Chicken, 44
  Pineapple Glazed Chicken, 48
  Roast Chicken with Noodles, 49
  Soy-Garlic Glazed Chicken, 48
  Stuffed Chicken Italiano, 50
  Vegetable-stuffed Chicken, 45
Wild Rice,
  Quick Chicken & Wild Rice Soup, 58
  Wild Rice Casserole, 73
Wine,
  Chicken in Lemon-Wine Sauce, 22
  Coq Au Vin, 25